TEMPORALITY AND TRINITY

Temporality and Trinity

Peter Manchester

Fordham University Press

NEW YORK ‡ 2015

Fordham University Press has no responsibility for the persistence or accuracy of URLs for external or third-party Internet websites referred to in this publication and does not guarantee that any content on such websites is, or will remain, accurate or appropriate.

Fordham University Press also publishes its books in a variety of electronic formats. Some content that appears in print may not be available in electronic books.

Visit us online at www.fordhampress.com.

Library of Congress Cataloging-in-Publication Data available online at catalog.loc.gov.

Printed in the United States of America
17 16 15   5 4 3 2 1
First edition

CONTENTS

ABBREVIATIONS

BPP   Heidegger, *The Basic Problems of Phenomenology*
BT   Heidegger, *Being and Time*
CSSL   Corpus Christianorum Series Latina
DT   Augustine, *De trinitate*
GA   Heidegger, Gesamtausgabe
GPP   Heidegger, *Grundprobleme der Phänomenologie*
LSJ   Liddell, Scott, Jones, Greek Lexicon
NPNF   Nicene and Post-Nicene Fathers
OT   Augustine, *On the Trinity* (trans. A. West Hadden)
ST   Manchester, *The Syntax of Time*
SZ   Heidegger, *Sein und Zeit*
Trin. Augustine, *On Trinity* (trans. E. Hill)

TEMPORALITY AND TRINITY

Introduction

THE PROJECT

HEIDEGGER IN *BEING AND TIME* positions himself in theology expertly, and often profoundly. It is no longer out of the question to look for theological implications in the Heidegger of that period. But it has not yet been widely recognized that the ecstatic-horizonal temporality of chapters 3 and 4 of the second division, which "arrives at the last minute" as Theodore Kisiel puts it,[1] has a theological background, and its particular dogmatic context has hardly been noticed at all.

That background is Augustine's treatise *On Trinity*. More precisely, it is the structure of its temporal problematic, which is trinitarian. As early as *Confessions*, Augustine had an ecstatic understanding of memory (his way of addressing having-been-ness). But in *On Trinity,* an ecstatic experience of the future, of freedom, of will (*voluntas*, the voluntary) not only becomes thematic, but also takes on a leading role in the structure or pattern of unity of the phenomenological threesome itself (*memoria, intelligentia, voluntas*), which has far-reaching implications for the ontologies of human being-toward-God and divine being-toward-creation, above all toward the human within creation.

To put the future in the first place so decisively is Augustine's way of responding to the apocalyptic character of revelation in the New Testament, and in particular to Paul's vision of the apocalyptic (1 Cor. 15): "in an instant" (*en atomô*), "in the twinkling of an eye" (*en ripê ophthalmou*) "we shall all transform" (taking *allagêsometha* to be middle

---

1. Theodore Kisiel, *The Genesis of Heidegger's* Being and Time, University of California Press, 1993, 7.

voice).[2] As a matter of dogmatic theology, the ecstatic-temporal trinity reveals the being of the human, because it reflects the special status of the human creature as *imago dei*, the image of the divine life, of Father and Son in one Spirit. Revelation is consummated in the disclosure space these two trinities share, the one ecstatically, the other transcendently.

By taking the "created in the image of God" of Genesis 1:26 to imply that the human being is a trinity, Augustine not only takes an innovative position in anthropology, but in theology itself. He shifts the designation of the phrase "God the creator" from the Father (to whom it was applied by consensus among the Greek Fathers, and arguably in the New Testament itself) to the "whole" trinity; i.e., to the Father and Son and Spirit acting as one. In the history of systematic Christian theology, there is a deep disagreement as to whether trinity or Christology is the dogmatic home of fundamental theology; i.e., elucidation of the New Testament as revelation. Thomas Aquinas notably adheres to a Christological systematics: the three moments of the *Summa Theologiae* are: i) God and the creature as from God; ii) the moral creature as ordered to God and to union with him; and iii) Christ the mediator. This is a scheme shaped by the problematic of mediation, one that routinely veers off into metaphysics. Augustine's, by contrast, is the paradigm of a trinitarian position in fundamental theology. Here the guiding problematic is revelation itself, the essence of its truth.

With regard to the ontology of divine life, the deepest question left open by Augustine is whether God *is* as he is *revealed*. How that question arises in *On Trinity* requires (and will receive) extensive elaboration in chapter 2, "The Temporality of Trinity in Augustine." What needs to be noted here is that, philosophically, the argument of Books VIII through XIV of that treatise proceeds in the dimension of *time and eternity*, taken as a single topic. In chapter 1 ("The Temporal Problematic of *Being and Time*"), I will show how, under influence of Kierkegaard, Heidegger in his own way acknowledges that "time and eternity" are essentially one topic, not two, so that temporality is the disclosure space of their difference. That *temporality* (the threesome future, past, present) is not *time* (infinite succession, supporting only the binary ordering difference

2. 1 Cor. 15:51–52. So also, I will argue, *metamorphoumetha* in 2 Cor. 3:18. Full discussion in chapter 2.

before/after), but follows from something like a "synthesis" of time with eternity, is of course Kierkegaard's claim in chapter 3 of *The Concept of Angst*, to which Heidegger devotes three separate footnotes. A fourth footnote points beyond Kierkegaard to the theological dimension of the time-and-eternity problem itself, at the level of consequence it has in Augustine.

> If God's eternity can be "construed" philosophically, then it can be understood only as a more primordial temporality that is "infinite." Whether the way afforded by the *via negationis et eminentiae* is a possible one, remains to be seen.[3]

Why Heidegger should be aware of that level of consequence is apparent from a passage in the two chapters of Dilthey's *Einleitung in die Geschichtswissenschaften* that he copied by hand in 1918, during the period leading up to his "coming out" as a free Christian and no longer a Catholic theologian. Dilthey is summarizing what is important about Augustine as a historical figure, and finds it in the centrality he gives to inwardness and self-awareness.

> In this awareness, the very essence of *his self* occurs to a human, and his conviction of the reality of the *world* is at least assigned its place; above all, the essence of *God* is apprehended in that awareness. Indeed, it seems to half uncover even the mystery of the Trinity.[4]

This is transparently an allusion by Dilthey to the argument of *On Trinity* VIII–XIV, as Heidegger will have recognized.

I want to argue that there is a deep homology between the roles of temporal problematic in Augustine, *On Trinity,* and Heidegger, *Being and Time.* My claim is not that Heidegger is under the influence of *On Trinity.* Even though his awareness of that treatise can be established, the movement of thought in this project is the reverse of tracking influences. I move from the temporal problematic of *Being and Time* to the

---

3. SZ 427n, BT 499n xiii.

4. *Einleitung in die Geschichtswissenschaften* 260, *Introduction to the Human Sciences* 234f. Cited by Kisiel, *Genesis* 103.

psychological explication of the human image of God in *Trinity*, schematized as memory, understanding, and will. Formal and phenomenological parallels allow me to interpret that psychological triad as a temporal problematic in the manner of *Being and Time*. In a sense, this is to say that I read Augustine as influenced by Heidegger. But my aim is more constructive than that. I believe that establishing a link between trinitarian theology and *Being and Time* opens a much more direct way of benefitting from it in theology than do some of Heidegger's own assumptions at the time. It puts me in a position to confront New Testament theology directly, in its own historicality, without digression into anything like "philosophy of religion."

There is no indication that Heidegger was drawn in the direction of trinitarian theological thinking. I believe that he was held back from the theological potential of ecstatic-horizonal temporality by his deep roots in medieval Catholic thinking and by its approach to Aristotle. Even in working against it, there is in *Being and Time* a dependence on scholasticism and a tendency to revert to a scholastic Christological scheme for fundamental theology, as evidenced by the role of the dyad "finite/infinite" underlying the cited footnote. Instead of speaking of finite temporality versus infinite temporality, a more productive use of the horizonal schemata would hold that while the human lives ecstatically into those horizons, the divine lives transcendingly into the same horizons.

THE PLAN

Chapter 1, "The Temporal Problematic of *Being and Time*," will clarify a topic beset by considerable confusion, indicate reasons for the confusion (rooted in uncertainty about the relation between the two divisions of the published work), and introduce what I mean by saying that, schematically, Heidegger's approach to temporality is trinitarian.

While it will take the whole of chapter 2, "The Temporality of Trinity in Augustine," to clarify everything that I mean by "trinitarian," the temporal schematism of the second division of *Being and Time* is trinitarian in the simplest of senses in that it is formally triadic. But *four* existentialia arise in the existential analytic of the first division, and little in their exposition seems to look toward a triadic schematism. To the contrary, many who would look for the temporal problematic of *Being and Time* in the final chapters of the first division, find it in the twofold structure thrown-projection. In chapter 1, I will test whether this is a clue that something new and perhaps rather sudden arrives with tri-horizonal ecstatic temporality. I will also explore the specifically trinitarian implications of the priority Heidegger assigns to the future in the unity of the ecstasies.

Chapter 1 also presents my unexpected discovery that Heidegger's time "as commonly understood" (*vulgäre Zeitbegriff*) does not in fact arise from his interpretation of Aristotle's treatise on time, but is a construct of his own, arising from a feature of world-time (*Weltzeit*) called "datability" (*Datierbarkeit*), a triadic pattern deriving from ecstatic-horizonal temporality. Heidegger's effort to attach his construct to Aristotle's "definition of time" (number of motion) reflects several oversights and misunderstandings of the treatise, and this has made its own contribution to uncertainty about the temporal problematic.

Chapter 2 will establish the temporality of trinity in Augustine by juxtaposing the temporal interpretation of the care-structure in *Being and Time* with a phenomenological interpretation of Augustine's psychological schema for the trinitarian image of God as memory, understanding, and will. By tracing Augustine's distinctive approach to memory back to its first appearance, in *Music*; its ripening, in *Confessions* X; and its role as figure for the Father, in *On Trinity*, I will show that the psychological image is not only a *temporal* triad, but that it is *ecstatic* as well.

Because of the way Augustine uses the image of God theme, this result permits the horizons of temporality to pertain directly to *revelation*, not just in systematic theology, but in the New Testament itself. Chapter 3, "Trinity in the New Testament," presents the insights I have gained in New Testament theology in recent years that are the principal basis of this project.

THE GOAL

The proposition "Dasein is the *imago dei*" is not susceptible to confirmation from literary influence or formal analogies between arguments in Heidegger's book and Augustine's. It is a proposition in fundamental theology, and can only be tested by exploring its productivity in the hermeneutics of the New Testament. Hence chapter

3, "Trinity in the New Testament" will leave behind both Augustine's treatise *On Trinity* and Heidegger's project *Being and Time*, and turn to the gospels—specifically, to what is perhaps the deepest mystery they present, how to include both Mark and John in the same bible. How does the apocalyptic futurity that provides the context for the trinitarian epiphany of the baptismal icon in Mark cohere with the "realized eschatology" of the trinitarian Last Supper discourse in John, in which the eternal Son is heard speaking in that office, present as the one who said, "Before Abraham came to be, I am" (John 8:58)?[5]

In the years leading up to *Being and Time*, Heidegger was aware of "historical Jesus" research, and of the crisis created for dogmatics by challenges to the historicity of the gospel narratives, but he shows great reserve in that period toward the gospels and Jesus, preferring to engage Paul and to orient the hermeneutical-phenomenological "move to experience" toward "primitive Christianity," and his existential analytic to the response of faith to the proclamation of the resurrection. The sense of that move, as Heidegger appropriated it from Yorck/Dilthey, is to root questions of historicity in historicality, the truth of existence itself—that toward which form-criticism points in asking about the *Sitz im Leben* of the discoverably various "forms" that the Jesus tradition took as it moved toward its literary embodiment in the gospels.

I spoke of reserve in respect to the narrative gospels because as a matter of methodological necessity, the move to experience here has to be to the experience of Jesus and his discipleship, between baptism and entombment. If this is to be available to us, we will need a link, an interior connection to that discipleship, for which the debates about historicity are not useful. They give us no access to two positions the New Testament takes in fundamental theology, positions that arise from its presentation of Jesus and become the doctrines of "resurrection" and "incarnation." In chapter 3, I will argue that the *Sitz im Leben* of these foundational *theologoumena* of Christian dogmatics is *eucharist*, the blessing and table fellowship that links the discipleship of Jesus on the

---

5. *prin Abraam genesthai, egô eimi.* This is almost invariably mistranslated (including in the RSV) as "before Abraham was, I am." This not only misses the aspect difference between the narrative aorist and the present tense, it abandons the lexical difference between the verbs *gignomai* and *eimi*.

way to the cross with the communities of prayer that emerged afterward. The "continuity" of that link is the temporal disclosure space—the "having-been-ing present-ifying future"—in which divine life and its image reach into every today. The burden of chapter 3 is therefore to show how only trinitarian theology and its coordinate temporal problematic allow us to uncover the eucharistic continuity between the apostolic Christianity of the synoptic gospels and the gnosis-Christianity of John's Gospel. In the very structure of this tradition liturgically, its derivation from the historical discipleship and table blessing of Jesus is implicated.

1. The Temporal Problematic
of *Being and Time*

THERE IS PARALYZING CONFUSION about what the temporal problematic of Martin Heidegger's *Being and Time* actually is. "Ecstatic-horizonal temporality" is of fundamental importance for the treatise. About that there is no uncertainty at all. But there is no wide agreement as to how that importance is to be identified. How temporality, the theme of Division Two of the published work, coheres with the phenomenology of being-in-the-world in Division One, remains an open question.

I will address features of the published work itself that contribute to this confusion shortly. But I must first confront the question why, given that we are engaging a treatise entitled "Being and *Time*," we are talking about *temporality* instead. Since completing my 1972 dissertation, *The Doctrine of the Trinity in Temporal Interpretation*,[1] it has been a fundamental conviction of mine that temporality and time must be strongly differentiated, not just terminologically but as phenomenal domains. "Temporality" refers to future, past, and present, "time," to a concomitant of sensible motion most familiarly addressed as succession. Future, past, and present are in no way timelike. In no way do they succeed each other, or come into any order. They are not *parts* of time, not directions along a time-line, and their unity is not based on time.

Until very recently, I assumed that Heidegger distinguishes the two phenomenal domains in a similar way. He does not. He means by "temporality" just what I do. But I have come to judge that he is fundamentally confused about physical time, as comes out in his reading

1. Graduate Theological Union, Berkeley, Ph.D. in Systematic and Philosophical Theology.

8

of Aristotle's treatise on time (*Physics* IV, 10–14). Such a charge plainly calls for exposition and defense, which it will receive below. But here at the start, it helps me explain how the "time" of Heidegger's title has become so beset by terminological noise that it is he himself, and not just faulty readings of his argument, that is the chief source of the confusions I hope to clear away in this chapter.

Basically, in *Being and Time* Heidegger no longer means anything in particular by the word "time," but rather defines it differently in the two main contexts in which he uses it. As the theme announced by his title, he stipulates that he means *primordial* time (*ursprüngliche Zeit*). When he otherwise refers to "time," he qualifies it "as commonly understood" (*vulgäre Zeitbegriff*). He does not approach this latter "time" in relation to motion, but offers a construct of his own he calls "now-time" (*Jetzt-Zeit*). From my point of view, therefore, he does not have a position on physical time at all.

In place of the ungainly "primordial time," Heidegger mostly just speaks of *temporality* (*die Zeitlichkeit*). In his writing, the term stands on its own as a noun. It is not the temporality *of* anything. In particular, it is not the temporality of Dasein.[2] It cannot even be said to "be"; instead it "brings itself about" (*sich zeitigt*).[3] It brings about that for any entity, the meaning of its being must be projected in the horizons of futurity, having-been, and present, in the pattern of their unity.

I have long been comfortable with thinking that temporality is like this, because four years before I first read *Being and Time* in a graduate seminar, I spent an undergraduate semester on Søren Kierkegaard's *Begrebet Angest* (*The Concept of Anxiety*). To open this chapter, I will summarize Kierkegaard's way of distinguishing temporality from time in that work, and place it in the context of his larger argument. Three separate footnotes in *Being and Time* praising specifically that work amply justify privileging it as a doorway into temporal problematic.

2. Heidegger muddies the water here by referring to authentic and inauthentic temporality in §64, when, strictly speaking, it is only Dasein that is authentic or inauthentic.

3. I make no attempt to preserve the wordplay of *die Zeitlichkeit sich zeitigt* by translating "temporality temporalizes itself," because I have no idea what "temporalize" might mean.

TEMPORALITY, ANXIETY, AND GUILT IN KIERKEGAARD

In most writers, it is unnecessary to decide whether the words "temporal" (*zeitlich*) and "time" (*Zeit*) differ in denotation more significantly than as an adjective trivially derived from a noun. But in *Being and Time*, there is a profound difference between temporality and time. Kierkegaard seems to have been the first to hint at such a specialization of the word "temporality," for reasons worth exploring in some detail.

Kierkegaard calls *Anxiety* "a simple psychologically orienting deliberation on the dogmatic issue of hereditary sin."[4] The accomplishment on which I shall focus amounts to a transcendent-temporal interpretation of the soul's relation to the divine eternity: that is, a metaphysical theory or doctrine of the soul. Yet it is also a recognizable precursor to empirical psychology, the empirical and metaphysical aspects coming together in the concept of "inwardness." The temporal character of this psychology arises from its phenomenological focus on what Kierkegaard calls the "moment" (*Øjeblikket*, like German *Augenblick*, the "twinkling of an eye").

> The moment is that ambiguity in which time and eternity touch each another. With this the concept of *temporality* is posited, whereby time constantly intersects eternity and eternity constantly pervades time, and, as a result, the above-mentioned division acquires its significance: the present time, the past time, the future time.[5]

This psychology is oriented to the theological problem of hereditary sin. Here the metaphysical scope of the discussion allows Kierkegaard to formulate a position on a problem that had not been treated explicitly in psychology since the great cosmological psychologies of late antiquity: namely, the unity of the life of the individual with the life of the race. Meditating on the Genesis account of the Adam's sin, he confronts us not four pages into his treatise with the perfectly serious affirmation that the individual *is* the race, and the race also the individual.[6] Walter

---

4. *The Concept of Anxiety*, edited and translated by Reidar Thomte and Albert B. Anderson. Princeton University Press, 1980, 1. Hereafter, *Anxiety* 1.

5. *Anxiety* 89.

6. *Anxiety* 28. "man is *individuum* and as such simultaneously himself and the whole race, and in such a way that the whole race participates in the individual, and the individual in the whole race."

Lowrie, in his translator's introduction to the older translation, *The Concept of Dread*, writes with some understatement:

> It is very interesting that S. K. is the only modern man who has so profound a sense of the solidarity of the race that original sin makes any sense to him.[7]

The actual thesis posits more than solidarity, of course, and in order to make it intelligible, Kierkegaard considers how to think about history "psychologically."

The psychological question about Adam in his judgment is not "What was he thinking when he sinned?" but "When is it that Adam sins?" This interpretation of history, which puts Adam first in such a way that his becomes chronologically the "first sin," subordinates the freedom of individual members of the race to the single action of an individual, whose freedom before God thus so far outstrips that of subsequent individuals that he is in effect placed "outside the race." Such an interpretation of history has no room for Adam.

Kierkegaard maintains that Adam commits sin at the same time, that is to say in the same historical "when," as any individual. Adam does what "the man" does, in a history that each of us embodies in our own biography. The question "When does Adam sin?" becomes for him not a matter of chronology or the assignment of dates, nor in fact a matter of any phenomena displayed along linear time. It is rather a matter of "What makes up a 'when'?" What sorts of "whens" are there in a life?

As soon as he has the question in this form, he can give the answer that provokes his philosophical psychology. He formulates: "Hereditary sin enters in an moment of anxiety (*Angst*)."[8] Any philosophical interpretation of a Christian consciousness of sin (and therefore of freedom) must understand how to generate the psychological concept of the *moment* and why to restrict the illustration of this concept to the

---

7. *The Concept of Dread*, translated by Walter Lowrie (Princeton University Press, 1957), xi. This is still my favorite translation, though Thome and Anderson are importantly more accurate for our topic.

8. Abridgment of the argument of chapter 1, §6, *Anxiety* 46–51.

mood of *anxiety*. Both demands call for an appropriate understanding of temporality. Let me begin with the concept of the moment.

In preparation for the explicitly temporal form of his problematic, Kierkegaard first describes the moment of sin, the transition from innocence to guilt, as a "qualitative leap." This elegant but formalistic phrase indicates an alternative, under the category of "transition," to the ordinary idea of "succession in time."

The transition from innocence to guilt cannot be studied in a conscience that is innocent. If we determine to treat this transition in terms of before and after, we stand in need of a knowledge of innocence that is like our knowledge of guilt, and we fall into a new sin. The act of imagination that would think the qualitative leap from the side of innocence must therefore regulate itself by an absolutely unique dialectic. It must know about what it does not know.

Kierkegaard interprets this dialectic as the "dialectic of spirit," of soul and body brought together in expression of a life that transcends them. The uniqueness of the moment in which psychosomatic life attains the qualitative leap into freedom is to be explored by psychological meditation on the meaning of spirit.

The dialectical structure of Kierkegaard's interpretation of spirit is less Hegelian than first appears, with all the talk of "syntheses" and "positings." In essence, he is both recovering, and attempting a constructive reinterpretation of, the tripartite anthropology of antiquity that distinguished body from soul and both from mind or spirit. On the basis of modern dualistic mind-body anthropology, there is a strong tendency to think of the ancient anthropology as a "three-story" theory of man, but Kierkegaard renovates the schema in a most suggestive way. His basic dialectical premise is that "man is a synthesis of psyche and body that is constituted and sustained by spirit."[9] "Spirit" thus names a possible state of the body-soul unity. It is to be distinguished from another state of the unity, the state he calls the "sensuous." The problem of synthesizing body and soul does not here amount to the metaphysical problem of combining the "two substances" of the Cartesian position, as though either could be discovered by itself. Instead, there are two different syntheses or lives in which psychosomatic existence can be

9. *Anxiety* 81.

sustained. The first, in which Kierkegaard says "the spirit is dreaming," is the sensuous immediacy of the life of nature. The second, in which the spirit is awake and self-possessed, is freedom, the life for which sin, guilt, repentance, and salvation have significance.

The dialectic of spirit must be developed in such a way that the *antecedent guilt* of we who formulate the problem is given its due. None of us illustrate the sensuous immediacy in the condition of innocence that scripture attributes to Adam in the garden. Yet it is precisely in the transition *from innocence* to guilt that we must portray the essence of freedom. We must somehow contrive to interpret innocence without making the aesthetic and finally moral mistake of trying to think our way into it.

The solution for Kierkegaard is the psychological category of anxiety.

> In innocence man is not qualified as spirit but is psychically qualified in immediate unity with his natural condition. The spirit in man is dreaming. . . . In this state there is peace and repose; but there is simultaneously something else that is not contention and strife, for there is indeed nothing against which to strive. What, then, is it? Nothing. But what effect does nothing have? It begets anxiety.[10]

Anxiety is the "nothing" of spirit. It is a psychological state and can therefore be observed in psychosomatic life by reflective thought. It is accessible to "descriptive psychology" conceived as a science. Yet as the shadow of spirit, a symptom that exposes psychosomatic life as "dreaming spirit," anxiety illustrates and guards by its profound ambiguity the conscientious reticence in which Christian consciousness reflects on freedom. Anxiety is "a sympathetic antipathy and an antipathetic sympathy."[11] Most of the argument in the first two chapters of *Anxiety* elaborates, through a kind of representative biography of the soul, the experience of being in anxiety as one approaches the moment of the qualitative leap. Kierkegaard's brilliance lies in demonstrating how heresies in the hermeneutic of the scriptural narrative about Adam correlate point for point with psychological oversimplification of the absolute ambiguity of anxiety.

10. *Anxiety* 41.
11. *Anxiety* 42.

Our concern with the dialectic of spirit has less to do with Kierkegaard's concrete elaboration of anxiety than with his ontology of the transcendence of spirit, which his psychology and the concept are meant to protect. Anxiety is alleged to be a psychological category that thought can follow up to the very instant where sin breaks out, where spiritual freedom is posited for man as actual. This is called "the moment." In order to interpret spirit's transcendence of the life of soul, Kierkegaard must show how the category of the moment transcends the sequence of moments of experience in which psychic life appears for scientific observation. Since this sequence is *time*, while the life of spirit is *eternal*, he is brought to a discussion of time and eternity.[12]

The "leap" from nothing to freedom is like no "transition" or becoming in time, since time is kept out of the dialectic between nothing and freedom. If by "history" we mean the sequence of events in which becoming-in-time takes on quasi-spatial "location" (for which Kierkegaard reserves the pejorative term "world-history"), then the moment is not in history, but history in the moment.

What Kierkegaard thinks of as transition or leap is related to what Heidegger calls an *ekstasis*. Freedom *ex-histêsi* (stands out from) nothing. An ecstasis is more like a situation than an event—in this case the situation of a very special kind of transcending. If it were necessary to describe how this situation comes about, a procedure which always confers an event-character on it, Kierkegaard would speak of the *synthesis of time and eternity*. The outcome of this event he calls *temporality*. With this term he is identifying the source of that explicit and theoretically motivated distinction between time and temporality required for the temporal problematic of *Being and Time*.

To see this, let us return to the formulation already cited:

The moment is that ambiguity in which time and eternity touch each another, and with this the concept of *temporality* is posited. . . . As a result, the above-mentioned division acquires its significance: the present time, the past time, the future time.

12. The opening pages of chapter 3, 81–93.

The moment is to be found in time, but it belongs to eternity. The mark of eternity on time is the "division" past, present, future. In order to show that these phenomena result from the time-eternity synthesis, Kierkegaard must demonstrate that they cannot be generated from the concept of time alone.

> If time is correctly defined as infinite succession, it most likely is also defined as the present, the past, and the future. This distinction, however, is incorrect if it is considered to be implicit in time itself; because the distinction only appears through the relation of time to eternity and through the reflection of eternity in time.[13]

To show the insufficiency of time, we need only reflect on the "correct" definition of time as infinite succession. It has two elements. Time is first of all succession, by which Kierkegaard means a category of transition. The nature of this transition is "going-by" or passing. As pure succession, time comprises a series of transitions from "present" to "past" in the sense of "gone." The other element of its definition identifies this series as infinite. "Infinite" here refers not to the "total length" of time but to the unlimited multiplicity of transitions into which the time-series may be sectioned. This rules out a "present," and therewith a past and future.

> If in the infinite succession of time a foothold could be found, i.e., a present, which was the dividing point, the division [into past, present, and future] would be quite correct. However, precisely because every moment, as well as the sum of the moments, is a process (a passing-by), no moment is a present, and accordingly there is in time neither present, nor past, nor future.[14]

Kierkegaard knows that by the "present" we never mean the absolutely punctual, but a more or less extended "length of time" like "today," "this week," "the present century." But as soon as we speak of time in terms of its length, we already presuppose the ecstatic point of

13. *Anxiety* 85.
14. *Anxiety* 85.

view from which such an essentially spatial characteristic can be discerned. Since only this ecstasy enters "presence," the equation of a length of time with the present destroys both concepts.

> If it is claimed that this division [past, present, future] can be maintained, it is because the moment is *spatialized*, but thereby the infinite succession comes to a halt, it is because representation is introduced that allows it to be represented instead of being thought. Even so, this is not correct procedure. For even as representation, the infinite succession of time is an infinitely contentless present (this is the parody of the eternal). The Hindus speak of a line of kings that has ruled for 70,000 years. Nothing is known about the kings, not even their names (this I assume). If we take this as an example of time, the 70,000 years are for thought an infinite vanishing; in representation it is expanded and spatialized into an illusionary view of an infinite, contentless nothing.[15]

In order to save the concept of time and of the present, we must appeal to an ecstatic phenomenon that attains presence while embedded in time. This is of course the moment. It confers presence upon time by being the synthesis of time and eternity, for:

> The present is the eternal, or rather the eternal is the present, and the present is full. In this sense the Latin said of the deity that he is *praesens* (*praesentes dii*), by which expression, when used about the deity, he also signified the powerful assistance of the deity.[16]

Presence in fullness and power is the essence of the "content" of which time by itself is void. The deftness with which the moment mediates between time and eternity is for Kierkegaard well captured in the figurative word for "moment": *Øjeblikket*, the "twinkling of an eye."

As soon as we let eternity awaken the moment out of time, we have temporality: the past, the present, and the future. Now Kierkegaard is ready to use the time-eternity synthesis to interpret the dialectic of spirit.

---

15. *Anxiety* 85–86.
16. *Anxiety* 86.

In that dialectic we distinguished two ways in which soul and body can be brought to unity of life: (1) the sensuous life of nature, and (2) the spiritual life of freedom. Each of these unities can be regarded as "posited" by spirit, the first as innocence or the "dream of the spirit," the second as the knowledge of good and evil or "spirit in history," finite freedom. To these two states of the psychosomatic life correspond the two kinds of "time": (1) linear successive time, the "when" of nature, and (2) temporality, the "when" of freedom. In the same way that spirit awakens freedom from sensuosity, eternity awakens temporality from time.

With this admittedly schematic summary of how Kierkegaard comes to adopt the term temporality to speak of past, present, and future in distinction from time, I will leave off further exposition of his argumentation in *Anxiety* and its sometimes exasperating complications. Even though I have only reached the introductory ten pages of chapter 3, "Anxiety as that Sin which is Default of the Consciousness of Sin," it is already evident that if there is such a thing as a "temporal problematic" in *Anxiety*, it includes very much more than simply terminology.

TEMPORALITY IN THE PROGRAM OF *BEING AND TIME*

Programmatically, *Being and Time* makes a kind of wager: it proposes that temporality provides the horizon for the meaning of being *in any case of it*. Leaving aside for the moment the question why the wager is first tested on finite human historical existence (Dasein), the impetus for my dissertation research forty years ago was a conviction that temporality is also the horizon in which the meaning of the being of divine life (Father and Son in one Spirit) could be projected, providing a second confirmation of *Being and Time*'s thesis.

My formulation of *Being and Time*'s thesis as a wager is meant to reinforce what I said at the beginning: temporality stands on its own, as a noun. It is not the temporality *of* anything. In particular, and again, it is not the temporality of Dasein. Temporality has to be "bigger than Dasein" if it is to be the "upon which" of a projection of Dasein in its possible totality, authenticity, and unity in the care-structure—i.e., if it is the horizon of the meaning of its being. Consider the final sentences of *Being and Time*:

The existential-ontological constitution of Dasein's totality is grounded in temporality. Hence some primordial way in which ecstatical temporality itself brings-about must make possible the ecstatic projection of Being in general. How is this mode of the bringing-about of temporality to be Interpreted? Is there a way which leads from primordial *time* to the meaning of *Being*? Does *time* itself manifest itself as the horizon of *Being*?[17]

Here we see temporality clearly used with the absolute force on which I have been insisting, but in order to carry this summary of the state of the question back into contact with his title, Heidegger must reprise its qualification as *primordial* time.

In Chapter II of the introduction to *Being and Time,* Heidegger seems to distinguish systematically between temporality, *Zeitlichkeit*, and a Latinate coinage, *Temporalität* (with adjectives differentiated in parallel, *zeitlich* and *temporal*). Beyond the conundrum this presents for translators, there is no settled account of how systematically consequential the distinction is, much less what it actually signifies. Is there supposed to be something like a "temporalogical difference"?

The *Zeitlichkeit/Temporalität* distinction looms large in Intro. II, but it disappears altogether thereafter.[18] That it returns in Heidegger's 1927 lecture course "Basic Problems of Phenomenology," only increases the interest I take in the question why it plays no role in *Being and Time.* The

17. Martin Heidegger, *Sein und Zeit*, 12te Auflage. Tübingen: Max Niemeyer Verlag, 1972. *Being and Time*, translated by John Macquarrie and Edward Robinson. New York and Evanston: Harper and Row, 1962. I will give references in the order SZ 437, BT 488, because I will often diverge from Macquarrie/ Robinson on certain details. But in general I stay close to their translation, and in citing them I will generally abide by their capitalization strategy for marking distinctions like Being (*das Sein*) and being/entity (*Seiendes*), Interpret (*interpretieren*) and interpret (*auslegen*), though I will not follow it in my own text.

18. Sections 5, 6, and 8. It disappears thereafter, with a single exception that proves the rule, this sentence from Division I, ch. 5: "The existential meaning of this understanding of Being cannot be satisfactorily clarified within the limits of this investigation except on the basis of the Temporal (*temporal*) Interpretation of Being" (section 31, SZ 147, BT 188), which clearly refers back to the Introduction, ch. 2.

answer, I believe, is that it is the absolute use of the term "temporality" itself that marks the full arrival of the temporal problematic of *Being and Time*.

This can be seen immediately by comparing the published *Being and Time* with 1924's "The Concept of Time." In both the Marburg lecture and the longer monograph, the key assertion is that "Dasein is time" or that "time is Dasein."

> Da-sein, conceived in its most extreme possibility of be-ing, is *time itself*, not *in* time.[19]

> But how do we get from this Dasein, which we have explicated in terms of its authentic existence in the form of possibility, to time? We are already there. Time has been the object of constant consideration in the present study. By describing the ontological characteristic of the being of explorative running-ahead, we have already laid bare the phenomenon of time in terms of its genuine being. *Each Dasein is itself time*.[20]

This time is already temporality, in the sense that it is future, past, and present, and indeed already in the pattern of unity familiar from *Being and Time*.

> In forerunning Dasein *is* its future, in such a way that in this being futural, it comes back to its past and present.[21]

But this is not yet called temporality—or rather, when it is (once, at the end of the Marburg lecture), the context reinforces that this is the

---

19. "The Concept of Time" (Marburg lecture), in *Becoming Heidegger,* edited by Theodore Kisiel and Thomas Sheehan. Evanston: Northwestern University Press, 2007, 208.

20. *"Das jeweilige Dasein selbst ist (die) Zeit." The Concept of Time* (monograph), translated by Ingo Farin with Alex Skinner. London and New York: Continuum, 2011. *Der Begriff der Zeit*, Gesamtausgabe 64. Frankfurt am Main: Vittorio Klostermann, 2004. This reference is CT 47; BZ 57.

21. *Becoming Heidegger* 208.

temporality of Dasein, rooted in a decidedly adjectival relationship to Dasein.

> Da-sein is always in one of its possible modes of being temporal (*seines möglichen Zeitlichseins*). Da-sein is time, time is temporal. Dasein is not time, but temporality (*Zeitlichkeit*). The fundamental assertion, time is temporal, is therefore the most authentic determination. . . . Da-sein is its being gone, it is its possibility in forerunning to this being gone. In this forerunning I am properly time, I have time. In so far as time is in each instantiation mine, there are many times. *The* time is meaningless; time is temporal.[22]

In the longer working out of the monograph, this being-temporal, *Zeitlichsein*, "temporalness" as its translators nicely render it, starts to carry more weight as a noun than *Zeit* itself, and even to give over on occasion to temporality, *Zeitlichkeit*.

> The genuine being of Dasein is temporalness (*Zeitlichsein*). After all, Dasein is the 'time' that *exists* in the mode of temporalness (*Zeitlichsein*); the being of Dasein is temporality (*Zeitlichkeit*).[23]

The almost experimentally ventured use of temporalness and temporality at the end of the Marburg lecture has become pervasive in the monograph. One clear reason for this is that in order to hold onto the provocative formulation "Dasein itself is time," Heidegger has had to introduce a usage of "time" in scare quotes, in order to address what he will later call "world-time," the time of concernful dealings in the with-world and the use of clocks Already in 1924 we see him becoming terminologically self-conscious in this area. But there are no anticipations yet of the dramatic development we see in *Being and Time*, where temporality becomes something of its own, no longer the being of Dasein, but what brings it about that Dasein's being has meaning.

This is a critical point, and one I believe has remained unobserved. So very much of the phenomenology of Dasein in *Being and Time* is

---

22. *Becoming Heidegger* 212.
23. CT 51; BZ 61.

already sketched out in *The Concept of Time* that the new development is all too easy to overlook. It is most directly coordinate with two other programmatically important decisions: (i) association of the existentials that make up the care-structure (projective understanding, disposition [*Befindlichkeit*], and falling) with *horizonal schemata*: ahead-of-itself, already-in, being-alongside, and (ii) their interpretation as "ecstasies." These will be discussed in the section that follows. But I think there is evidence to support my impression that having Kierkegaard's usage in his ear explains in part why Heidegger lets temporality evolve into its new role.

He already references *Anxiety* in 1924, *The Concept of Time*, but only in the context of Kierkegaard's assertion that the "object" of anxiety is Nothing.[24] That same connection is acknowledged again in the first of the three references to *Anxiety* in *Being and Time*, in a note that has in view the whole of §40, "The basic disposition of anxiety as a distinctive way in which Dasein is disclosed." Here Heidegger goes on to say that anxiety and fear have come within the purview of Christian theology "ontically, and even (though within very narrow limits) ontologically:" This happens "when the anthropological problem of man's being toward God has won priority," which he illustrates first with references to Augustine and Luther, then concludes:

> The man who has gone farthest in analyzing the phenomenon of anxiety—and again in the theological context of a 'psychological' exposition of the problem of original sin, is Søren Kierkegaard. Cf. *Der Begriff der Angst*, 1844.[25]

This importantly broadens the reference to include the theological context, but with no hint yet that there is contact between temporality in Kierkegaard and his own temporal problematic.

The second reference is much more telling. The note attaches to §45, the prospectus for the whole of Division Two, "Dasein and Temporality."

---

24. CT 34n.

25. SZ 190n, BT 492n iv. The note goes on to cite the German edition of the *Gesamelte Werke* (Dedericks), vol. 5.

In the nineteenth century, Søren Kierkegaard explicitly seized on the problem of existence as an existentiell problem, and thought it through in a penetrating fashion. But the existential problematic was so alien to him that, as regards his ontology, he remained completely dominated by Hegel and by ancient philosophy as Hegel saw it. Thus there is more to be learned philosophically from his 'edifying' writings than from his theoretical ones—with the exception of the treatise on the concept of anxiety.[26]

Backhanded as the compliment may be, it expressly makes clear that he has "learned philosophically" from *Anxiety*, and, given the placement of the note, what he learned pertains to "Dasein and temporality."

The third and final reference is yet more specific. In chapter IV of Division Two, "Temporality and Everydayness," §68 "The temporality of disclosedness in general" opens with a subsection "a" addressing the temporality of understanding, which is futural. I discuss §68 in detail in the next section of this chapter, but for now, suffice it that Heidegger comes to a point in his discussion where he needs terms for the authentic present though he has not heretofore provided any. "That *Present* which is held in authentic temporality and thus is *authentic* itself, we call the *moment of vision (Augenblick)*." Macquarrie/Robinson's translation of the word by a phrase is helpful, because "in the moment," what is revealed for resolute Dasein is "the Situation," in which being-alongside is transformed from evasion into the embrace of positive possibilities. Heidegger says, "This term must be understood in an active sense, as an ecstasis."[27] At the end of the paragraph in which the term *Augenblick* is introduced, Heidegger attaches a note that begins:

> S. Kierkegaard is probably the one who has seen the *existentiell* phenomenon of the moment of vision with the most penetration; but this does not signify that he has been correspondingly successful in Interpreting it existentially.[28]

26. SZ 235n, BT 494n vi.

27. SZ 338, BT 387.

28. SZ 338n, BT 497n iii. I continue discussing this note line by line in what follows.

I interrupt transcription and discussion of the note to make two points. First, the reason why a subsection focused on the temporality of understanding, which is primarily futural, would include discussion of the authentic present (and the authentic past as well, which is "repetition"), is that futurity is one of the horizons of temporality, and temporality is an inherently unitary phenomenon, so that each of future, past, and present must be taken into account, no matter which takes the lead in relation to a particular existentiale. Second, we saw that for Kierkegaard the moment of vision and temporality were co-posited, lending support to my hypothesis that Heidegger's expanded sense of temporality in *Being and Time* took impetus from *Anxiety*.

As he moves toward this note before us, we see Heidegger returning to the proviso he included in the first reference to *Anxiety*, when he said that anxiety and fear had been discussed in Christian theology both ontically, and ontologically, "though within very narrow limits." Those limits relate to a distinction he makes in the paragraph to which the note attaches, after stipulating that the moment of vision must be understood actively, as an ecstasis.

> The moment of vision is a phenomenon which *in principle* can *not* be clarified in terms of the "now" (*dem Jetzt*). The "now" is a temporal phenomenon which belongs to time as within-time-ness: the "now" 'in which' something arises, passes away, or is present-at-hand. 'In a moment of vision' nothing can occur, but as an authentic Present or waiting-toward (*Gegen-wart*), the moment of vision permits it *first to encounter* what can be 'in a time' as ready-to-hand or present-at-hand.[29]

Returning to the note, we find Heidegger acknowledging that he has learned something from Kierkegaard's *Anxiety* about the moment of vision and temporality, but then proceeding to misrepresent how Kierkegaard argues. It is a very complex note. I will take it step by step. After asserting that Kierkegaard has not succeeded in interpreting the moment of vision existentially, the note continues:

> He clings to the ordinary conception of time, and defines the moment of vision with the help of "now" and "eternity."

29. SZ 338, BT 388, with modification of the final sentence.

This is fanciful. Kierkegaard never talks about "now." The time that, devoid of the moment, is therefore barren of temporality, is infinite succession, which has nothing to do with "now."

> When Kierkegaard speaks of 'temporality', what he has in mind is man's being-in-time (*in-der-Zeit-sein*).

This is specifically and explicitly what Kierkegaard does *not* have in mind, as I have tried to bring out.

> Time as within-time-ness knows only the "now"; it never knows a moment of vision.

This is pure assertion by Heidegger, unrelated to anything Kierkegaard talks about, as Heidegger seems to accept when he goes on with another backhanded compliment:

> If, however, such a moment gets experienced in an existentiell manner, then a more primordial temporality has been presupposed, though existentially it has not been made explicit.[30]

The argument seems to be that if we credit Kierkegaard with experiencing a moment of vision, existentiell, the most we can take him to mean by the 'temporality' he says is co-posited in the moment is within-time-ness. But by temporality Kierkegaard means something emergent in the coming together of time *and eternity*. I cite again his passage:

> The moment is that ambiguity in which time and eternity touch each another, and with this the concept of *temporality* is posited, whereby time constantly intersects eternity and eternity constantly pervades time. As a result, the above-mentioned division acquires its significance: the present time, the past time, the future time.[31]

30. The footnote concludes by referring also to the discussion of Kierkegaard's "moment" in Jaspers, *Psychologie der Weltanshauungen*, 108ff., and to the "review of Kierkegaard," 419–32. These page references are still correct for the sixth edition. In his discussion of Kierkegaard's "moment," Jaspers paraphrases very accurately, and cites in its entirety the passage I repeat next. The word *jetzt* does not occur in his discussion.

31. *Anxiety* 89.

In the moment, the psychosomatic concretion of human life is brought into the synthesis of spirit, the event Kierkegaard calls the qualitative leap of freedom. The whole point here is that freedom does not belong to within-time-ness. It is exactly to guard the ecstatic character of the moment and the qualitative leap that Kierkegaard champions the profound ambiguity of anxiety, its sympathetic antipathy and antipathetic sympathy. Heidegger would have it that Kierkegaard defines the moment with the help of the "now" (which Kierkegaard does not even talk about), and "eternity"—about whose role Heidegger says nothing at all.

For all the garble in this note on Kierkegaard, Heidegger's reference to "a more primordial temporality" may be related to the distinction he puts forward in Introduction II, between *Zeitlichkeit* and *Temporalität*. That distinction seems to me to have been introduced after Division Two ("Dasein and Temporality [*Zeitlichkeit*]") was essentially completed. Far from making any contribution to the clarity or rigor of the temporal problematic of *Being and Time*, I believe it threatens to dismantle it. I will briefly state why.

Looking ahead to the relationship Division Two has to Division One, the "Preparatory Fundamental Analysis of Dasein," Heidegger writes in Introduction II:

> We shall point to *temporality* (*Zeitlichkeit*) as the meaning of the Being of that entity which we call "Dasein." If this is to be demonstrated, those structures of Dasein which we shall provisionally exhibit must be Interpreted over again as modes of temporality. In thus interpreting Dasein as temporality, however, we shall not give the answer to our leading question of the meaning of Being in general. But the ground will have been prepared for obtaining such an answer.[32]

The implication is that temporality is good enough for the meaning of the Being of Dasein, but not good enough for the meaning of Being in general. And sure enough, two pages later he writes:

---

32. SZ 17, BT 38.

Thus the fundamental ontological task of Interpreting Being as such includes working out the *Temporality of Being*. In the exposition of the problematic of Temporality (*Temporalität*) the question of the meaning of Being will first be concretely answered.[33]

If interpreting Dasein as temporality prepares the ground for the problematic of Temporality, how do we find our way from one to the other? In my view, this distinction is unnecessary and misleading. The position taken in Division Two holds that ecstatic-horizonal futurity (and with it, temporality as a whole) grounds not just the pre-ontological understanding of Dasein, but the pre-ontological understanding of Being in general.

In II, 3, after temporality has shown itself to be the meaning of the Being of Dasein, Heidegger concludes the chapter with a prospectus for the tasks still remaining in the Division (§66). These include an account of the temporality of everydayness (II, 4), an account of historicality (II, 5), and, finally, a demonstration of how time as ordinarily understood is founded on temporality (II, 6). Taking stock of where we will then be in the larger program of *Being and Time*, Heidegger ends the chapter saying:

> The existential-temporal analysis of Dasein demands, for its part, that it be repeated anew within a framework in which the concept of Being is discussed in principle.[34]

How can the existential-temporal analysis of Dasein be repeated anew in a framework where the concept of Being is discussed in principle, if temporality is taken apart into two problematics, the one "temporal" and the other "Temporal"? I return to the terms in which Heidegger touches on that "repeating anew" in the final words of the published treatise.

> The existential-ontological constitution of Dasein's totality is grounded in temporality. Hence some primordial way in which ecstatical temporality itself brings-about must make possible the ecstatic projection of Being in general. How is this mode of the bringing-about of temporality to be Interpreted? Is there a way which leads from

33. SZ 18, BT 40.
34. SZ 333, BT 382.

primordial *time* to the meaning of *Being*? Does *time* itself manifest itself as the horizon of *Being*?[35]

If we make the natural surmise that this "way" and the "repeating anew" that it entails was to be worked out in the missing Division Three, "Time and Being," then the terminological distinction Heidegger introduced late into Introduction II, between temporality and Temporality, is not a glimpse into the content of Division Three, but in its counter-productivity perhaps a hint about its ultimate suppression.

DASEIN AND TEMPORALITY

Temporality provides the horizon for the meaning of being *in any case of it*. A case of being (*Sachgebiet*) is called "entity" (*Seiendes*), and early in Introduction I, Heidegger gives an interesting list of such cases: "history, Nature, space, life, Dasein, language, and the like." These are adumbrations of what he there calls "*das All des Seienden*" (the All of entity).

> Being is always the Being of entity. The All of entity can, in accordance with its various domains, become a field for laying bare and delimiting certain definite areas of subject-matter (*bestimmte Sachgebiete*). These areas, on their part (for example, history, Nature, space, life, Dasein, language, and the like) can serve as objects which corresponding scientific investigations may take as their respective themes. Scientific research accomplishes, roughly and naively, the demarcation and initial fixing of the areas of subject-matter.[36]

35. SZ 437, BT 488.
36. SZ 9, BT 29, translation adapted. In SZ, *Seiendes* (entity) is almost always used in the singular. This is because it designates what Heidegger also calls a *Seinsweise, Seinsart,* or *Seinsmodus,* a manner of Being rather than "an entity" in the sense of "a thing." An especially important entity, for example, encountered within-the-world in concernful dealing, is entity ready-to-hand, *Zuhandenes.* In a familiar everyday context for concernful dealing, say a kitchen, there will be a sink, a stovetop, some knives, cutting boards, etc., but it is completely misleading to enumerate them and speak of the kitchen as teeming with "entities," because the *entity* (manner of Being) in question is an entity ready-to-hand, *equipment* (*Zeug*). Without denying the pluralities involved in any given network of assignments in a workplace, it nonetheless conduces to Heidegger's point that we can address them in a collective singular, as "gear" or equipment.

The inclusion of Dasein on that list could make it seem as though the complex priority of Dasein, (ontological/existential and ontical/existentiell), arises for "epistemological" reasons; i.e., that the scientific investigation of the All of entity should first study investigation itself and its competence. As though Dasein were simply selected from that list. That would misrepresent even Dasein's ontic priority. I shall not rehearse here the careful exposition of Dasein's priority in Introduction I, other than to say that without assent to the "Being-ontological" of existence,[37] trying to understand the temporal problematic of *Being and Time* would be pointless.

To say that a philosophical project incorporates a temporal problematic means that it explicitly addresses *the pattern* or *structure of the unity* of future, past, present. These, in their unity, we are calling *temporality*. Temporality is *not time*, nor is it in any way timelike (i.e., involving succession or order in that succession). Though future/past/present are in no way sequential, there is nonetheless situational precedence among them. For Heidegger, precedence goes to the future, to understanding analyzed as projection upon possibility. In the care-structure of I, 6, this precedence is met as existence itself, existentiality. Existentiality provides precisely the Open in which facticity engenders falling, having-been is basis for making-present.

This pattern, in which the future brings about the unity of the past and present and establishes a situational precedence between them in which making present is founded on having been, is captured in the formal definition of temporality Heidegger provides in II, 3:

> Coming back to itself futurally, resoluteness brings itself into the Situation by making present. The character of "having been" arises from the future, and in such a way that the future which "has been", *gewesene*, (better, which is "having-been-ing," *gewesende*), releases from itself the Present. This unitary phenomenon, set forth as a having-been-ing making-present future, we call *temporality*.[38]

By jumping directly to the definition of temporality in II, 3, I have left out of account anticipation (forerunning, *Vorlaufen*), resoluteness

37. SZ 12, BT 32.
38. SZ 326, BT 387, translation extensively adapted.

(*Entschlossenheit*), and the question of their unity, though these belong to temporal problematic in relation to the "ecstatic" and "horizonal" and will certainly be considered shortly. But whatever else may be true about future/past/present, *there are three of them*. The decidedly threefold pattern of ecstatic-horizonal temporality can seem ill-prepared-for if not actively disruptive when it finally arrives at the end of II, 3, because as we emerge from Division One, we have been provided with *four* equiprimordial factors in Dasein's existence. *Existentialia* Heidegger calls them: disposition (*Befindlichkeit*), understanding, discourse, and falling.

These are introduced, in that order, in I, 5, "Being-in as such." For a number of reasons, not just the non-matching "counts," there are sources of confusion over temporal problematic in that chapter in particular.

The first is to forget that I, 5 is not setting the stage for temporal interpretation. That is what happens in I, 6, "Care as the Being of Dasein," where the care-structure is threefold, as one would expect. I, 5 concludes the exposition of Being-in-the-world, Dasein's basic state, as a unitary phenomenon. Sketched in a preliminary way in I, 2, subsequent chapters treat the three items in its structure that Heidegger singles out for attention: world, "who," and Being-in. In "The Worldhood of the World" (I, 3), the general goal is to distinguish the world from anything like an object. In "Being-with and Being-Self" (I, 4), the goal is to prevent understanding the self or "who" is in the world as any kind of subject. So in I, 5 "Being-in as such," the goal is nothing like putting world and self together on analogy to "epistemology," but rather to exploit the fact that the "together" was thematized in advance of "world" and "self."

The master proposition in I, 5 is that *Dasein* is its own "*da*," Being-there is its own "there." "*Dasein is its disclosedness.*"[39] Now temporal problematic is a disclosure problematic, but not every disclosure problematic is directly a temporal one. This is especially germane in regard to the division of I, 5 into A and B sub-units. A is entitled "The existential Constitution of the 'there'," B "The everyday Being of the 'there', and the falling of Dasein." In previewing the structure of the chapter in §28, Heidegger addresses himself to A. as follows:

---

39. SZ 133, BT 171.

In *understanding* and *disposition*, we shall see the two constitutive ways of being the 'there'; and these are equiprimordial. If these are to be analyzed, some phenomenal confirmation is necessary; in both cases this will be attained by Interpreting some concrete mode which is important for the subsequent problematic. Disposition and understanding are characterized equiprimordially by *discourse*.[40]

It is very natural to look to the A section on the existential constitution of the "there" for what I earlier called the Open, for signs of the impending temporal problematic. And Heidegger has just referred to "*the two* ways of being the 'there'," and indicated that discourse provides phenomenal confirmation "*in both cases*."

The A section introduces two phenomena, disposition (*Befindlichkeit*) and understanding (*Verstehen*), each of which is characterized in vivid ways. Disposition, being found-out, having moods, belongs to Dasein's *thrownness,* while understanding is *projection*, projection upon possibility. They are explicitly taken together as "thrown projection" (§31), and the dynamism of the imagery can lead to premature and actively misleading ways of understanding the *ekstaseis* of ecstatic temporality. Disposition transparently relates to the past, understanding to the future, and a naive way of thinking about temporality can all too readily understand the "away-ness in time" that belongs to past and future as making them "ecstatic," whereas the present is just "here," hence not ecstatic at all. Heidegger prefers to speak of the past of thrownness as "having been," not past in the sense of passed or "away," and emphasizes that Dasein *is* its having been. In the same way, the possibilities upon which understanding projects itself futurally are not "away"; Dasein *is* its possibilities. Nonetheless, by identifying thrownness and projection as "the two" constitutive ways of being the "there," Heidegger invites misunderstanding.

A third existentiale is taken up in A: *discourse (Rede)*. Though it is not "counted" along with disposition and understanding in the care-structure, it is nevertheless equiprimordial with them. Discourse spins out of the analysis of understanding via a digression through interpretation into the apophantic intention of assertion, the historically

40. SZ 133, BT 171–72.

tenacious context for discussion of *logos*. The discussion represents yet another instance of Division One's efforts to take into account the traditional ontology of entity present-at-hand and "reality," not as having standing of its own, but as founded privitively upon concernful dealing, involvement, significance, and solicitude. It is in a way a kind of final review of that material.

Hence the disclosedness in view in the proposition that prevails in the A segment of I, 5, "Dasein is its disclosedness," is the disclosedness of the unitary basic state Being-in-the-world. It is not Dasein's temporal disclosedness, about which a parallel proposition, "Dasein is its temporality," would be wrong. Temporality is the disclosedness of Dasein's "is," the meaning of its being. In order to proceed into Division Two, we need an identification of that being, which Heidegger provides in the care-structure of I, 6, "Care as the Being of Dasein." The B section of I, 5 moves in that direction, "The everyday Being of the 'there', and the falling of Dasein." Throughout Division One, Heidegger has relentlessly insisted on explicitly taking into account how Dasein is, "first of all and mostly"; namely, in *everydayness*. This is the specific temporality of inauthenticity, and just as there is a naive thinking about temporality that can satisfy itself with just two "ecstasies" in A, there is a naive thinking about inauthenticity that does not see it as a disclosedness nor grasp how falling can be ecstatic.

Inauthentic (*uneigentlich*) means "not its own (*eigene*)." First of all and mostly, Dasein is a phenomenon not of its own manner of being but of entity encountered within-the-world, entity ready-to-hand or even simply present-at-hand. And its "who" is not its own self, but the "one," "anyone," "they," (*das Man*). Entity within-the-world is encountered in circumspective concern, and this is so far from a "negative" disclosedness of Dasein that it is precisely here that we confront what Heidegger calls Dasein's transcendence, its Being-alongside entity in such a way as to free it for its own proper discoverability.

Being-alongside is the ecstatic character of falling, just as ahead-of-itself is that of understanding, and already-in that of disposition. In I, 6 the priority of the future in the temporal triad is reflected by naming it existentially from existence itself, the original designation provided for the Being of Dasein. The character of being projectively ahead-of-itself is called *existentiality*. Being already-in, thrown and disposed, is called *facticity*. Being-alongside is called *falling*. In the care-structure, Dasein is existent, factical, and falling.

Care articulates the structural whole of Dasein, and I, 6 not only pulls that structure together, but also identifies the disclosure problematic within which temporal problematic properly unfolds: truth as unhiddenness *alêtheia*, (*a-lêtheia*), the truth of Being. It might seem that nothing further stands between us and an interpretation of existentiality, facticity, and falling in relation to futurity, having been, and making present, in the pattern of their unity in which the future is in the first place. However, in its disclosedness as articulated in the care-structure, Dasein is equiprimordially in the truth and in untruth, and in order for temporal interpretation to have the "purchase" necessary for the project of fundamental ontology, two issues arise that belong to temporal problematic ahead of tri-horizonal interpretation; Dasein's *totality* and its *authenticity*. These are treated respectively in II, 1, "Dasein's possible Being-whole, and Being toward death," and II, 2, "Dasein's attestation of an authentic can-be, and resoluteness."[41]

The discussion of being toward death in II, 1 is exceedingly familiar, but as a theme belonging to temporal problematic, certain implications need to be spelled out. In I, 5, in connection with understanding's character of projection (*Entwurf*) upon possibility, it was emphasized that Dasein *is* its possibilities. If in some sense these are "ahead," then Dasein *is this ahead*. So, too, with the possibility of death, for which Heidegger reserves the term "forerunning," "anticipation" (*Vorlaufen*). What is at stake in thinking this correctly is what will later be called the *ecstatic* character of temporality.

Death is the possibility of the impossibility of Dasein, yet manifestly belongs to any way in which Dasein can be a phenomenon in its totality. The term "forerunning"/ "anticipation" is meant to secure the uncanny logic of this situation, what in II, 2 will be called "being the null basis of

---

41. I have retranslated these titles. For II, 1, BT writes "Dasein's Possibility of Being-a-whole, and Being-toward-death," which reifies "possibility," and treats *Sein zum Tode* as though it were a compound word. In the title of II, 2, and throughout, BT translates *Seinkönnen* as "potentiality-for-Being." For a translation so formatted, I would prefer "capability for Being," since it is too easy to mix up "potentiality" and "possibility," but I find that "can-be" works fine.

a nullity." Even more seditiously than "projection," forerunning/ anticipation can convey a sense of movement in a "forward" direction, something common sense all but automatically associates with "the future." But in so far as there is anything like "motion" involved in Dasein's "having a future," the directionality is the reverse. Dasein runs ahead of itself "so fast" that it comes *toward* itself from out of a future that it *already is*. Ecstasis opens in the difference between being and nothing. It does not have to do with anything like spanning an expanse— of time, say. The same is true for the finitude of temporality, which has nothing to do with the fact that nobody lives forever.

For insight into the specifically temporal complications that arise with resoluteness and authenticity, it helps to notice a methodical reversal between Division One and Division Two, to which attention is not specifically drawn. Making a point that comes up again several times in I, 4, Heidegger writes:

> *Authentic Being-Self* does not rest upon an exceptional condition of the subject, a condition that has been detached from the 'they'; *it is rather an existentiell modification of the 'they'—of the 'they' as an essential existentiale*.[42]

There are two elements to this statement. It considers the *inauthentic* and the *authentic Self* to be connected by an *existentiell* modification, and it looks *from inauthenticity* toward authenticity. This is of a piece with the methodical demand throughout Division One that every analysis be carried out all the way into everydayness. In II, 3 however, we read,

> It has been shown that proximally and for the most part Dasein is *not* itself, but is lost in the they-self, which is an existentiell modification of the authentic Self.[43]

Once again, the authentic and the inauthentic self are connected by an existentiell modification, but here, we look from authenticity toward

42. SZ 130, BT 168, adapted.
43. SZ 317, BT 365.

inauthenticity. Nowhere in Division One is there a context for looking "in that direction." How has the context changed here in Division Two?

The remark comes early in §64, "Care and selfhood," the last preliminary before §65, "Temporality as the ontological meaning of care." Up to this point, II, 3 was concerned to bring together Dasein's possible totality in being toward death, established in II, 1, with its authenticity as manifested in resoluteness, expounded in II, 2, and to reflect on the hermeneutical situation that the treatise has reached.

Resoluteness (*Entschlossenheit*) is clearly a species of disclosedness (*Erschlossenheit*), and to keep it clear of connotations of willfulness, I think of it in optical terms, as "resolution" or "definition," as in high-definition television. What the moment of vision resolves is the situation, into which Dasein has been called back from its lostness in falling. It has been reached by the call of conscience, which summons it to its own-most being-guilty. In II, 2, the authentic can-be must above all be *attested existentiell*. The modification of the they-self must give us an authentic self, not just in a general way as existential possibility, but in a way that is attested factically, existentiell. In a famous passage, Heidegger describes a problem with this:

> Is there not, however, a definite ontical way of taking authentic existence, a factical ideal of Dasein, underlying our ontological Interpretation of Dasein's existence? That is so indeed. But not only is this Fact one which must not be denied and which we are forced to grant; it must also be conceived in its *positive necessity*, in terms of the object we have taken as the theme of our investigation.[44]

Perhaps there are hints at Heidegger's "factical ideal of Dasein" in *The Phenomenology of Religious Life*,[45] or in Christian theology more generally, but it is not supplied in *Being and Time*. Yet the demand that authentic self-being be attested concretely, factically, existentiell, cannot be renounced. This attestation is clearly and explicitly identified, though

44. SZ 310, BT 358.

45. *Phänomenologie des Religiösen Lebens*, GA 60, 1995. *The Phenomenology of Religious Life*, translated by Matthias Fritch and Jennifer Anna Gosetti-Ferencei. Bloomington and Indianapolis: Indiana University Press, 2004.

because of a misleading translation, it is almost always misunderstood. Heidegger names it with a giant Germanism, *Gewissenhabenwollen*, for which Macquarrie/Robinson write "wanting-to-have-a-conscience." This is almost inside-out. The proper sense is *"being willing* to have a conscience."

The call of conscience issues from Dasein's (possible) authenticity, which becomes factical when it is *heard*. "Wanting to have a conscience" would put the initiative on the side of the self of everydayness, as a sort of aspiration, which is the very thing that is missing in everydayness. The call of conscience issues entirely from the side of possible authenticity, and "being willing to have a conscience" does not purport to issue the call, but indicates only that it is heard. This is the threshold of authentic self-being, its existentiell attestation. Formally, it is nearly empty, but that is its virtue. No additional factical ideal of Dasein needs to be supplied. It is sufficient to bring us into the hermeneutical situation in which the self of everydayness can be grasped as an *existentiell modification of the authentic self*, reversing the direction of Division One.

In II, 3 the temporal interpretation of the care-structure ensues, and then is expanded to include consideration of all four existentialia in II, 4, "Temporality and Everydayness." I am going to postpone an account of the phenomenology involved to chapter 2, where the arguably analogous material in Augustine is also in view. For now, it suffices if we recognize the situations of precedence that obtain among future, having-been, and making-present, the structural importance within temporal problematic itself of forerunning toward death, and the nuance with which factical resolution and authenticity are introduced.

To conclude, I want to address the point I made at the beginning of the chapter, that strictly speaking there is no such thing as "authentic temporality" or "inauthentic temporality," there is just temporality. It is *Dasein* that is authentic or inauthentic, and these two possibilities are *brought about* by temporality. *Sed contra*, one could quickly amass fifty instances of Heidegger using the phrases I am opposing. If the distinction as I have just explained it is kept in mind, this is innocuous. But if it is taken as a back-door incursion of something like the *Zeitlichkeit /*
Temporalität distinction, that is something my whole account of temporal problematic rejects.

HEIDEGGER'S UNDERSTANDING OF PHYSICAL TIME

Near the end of *Being and Time*, Heidegger makes the signature remark that from any beginning within the concept of time (as ordinarily understood), "temporality is inaccessible in the reverse direction."[46] The context for this is the last chapter of Division Two, chapter 6, "Temporality and Within-time-ness as the source (*Ursprung*) of the ordinary time-concept," where he seeks to derive the ordinary time-concept from temporality. That derivation concludes in §81, "Within-time-ness and the genesis of the ordinary time-concept." Here his desire to attach himself to Aristotle's treatise on time in *Physics* becomes overt. He first summarizes his account of "now-time," and then presents it as an expansion of what he takes to be Aristotle's "definition (*Definition*) of time," which he cites as follows:

> *touto gar estin ho chronos, arithmos kinêseôs kata to proteron kai husteron*
> (Phys. IV, 11, 219b 1–2).

> This namely is time, what is counted in the movement encountered in the horizon of the earlier and later.[47]

I am comfortable enough with "encountered in the horizon of" for *kata*, but I call attention to the rather drastic transposition involved in translating *arithmos kinêseôs*, "the number (or count) of motion," as "what is counted in motion." As I shall argue below, this undoes the whole point of characterizing time as number, an association that was initially Old Pythagorean, and which is pivotal for Plato at *Timaeus* 37d, where time is an "image of eternity moving according to number." Time is the *number of* motion, its observable plurality. It is *motion* that gets numbered, not time.

I want to focus closely on Heidegger's resort to Aristotle's treatise on time. I have found Heidegger's understanding of the treatise surprisingly unsatisfactory. His reading is obtuse in that it ignores the passage directly preceding what he cites as the "definition of time," a passage that is of pivotal phenomenological importance. And when he presents "now-

---

46. SZ 426, BT 479.
47. SZ 421, BT 473, my translation of Heidegger's translation of Aristotle.

time," which he generates via "datability" from temporality, I find his exposition incoherent. This critique can be supported from II, 6 of *Being and Time* itself, but the engagement with Aristotle there is piecemeal at best. A much better foil is provided by *The Basic Problems of Phenomenology* (1927), §19 "Time and Temporality," where the "a" section includes an outline of the whole treatise on time, along with an interpretation of Aristotle's concept of time.[48] I will use this as a foil for my own account, rather than explicate it for its own sake.

A critique as drastic as this necessarily arises from a specific perspective, in this case my own account of Aristotle's treatise on time. I will therefore begin by revisiting key moments of my interpretation in the relevant chapter of *The Syntax of Time*.[49]

After announcing that he will turn next to the topic of time, Aristotle opens the treatise as follows:

> And first it bodes well to consider perplexities about it and to do so through exoteric reasonings, [asking]: (1) whether it is of things being or of things nonbeing, and then (2) what is its nature.[50]

An Aristotelian treatise quite routinely opens by considering "perplexities about its topic," but here Aristotle adds an extra characterization of his procedure: he will work "through exoteric reasonings" (*dia tôn exôterikôn logôn*). He might as well have said, "working from the *vulgäre Zeitbegriff*." Commonplace assumptions and ways of speaking about time raise questions that lead to irresolvable and

---

48. §19 is titled "Time and Temporality." It has an "a" section providing "Historical orientation regarding the traditional concept of time and a delineation of the common understanding of time that lies at the basis of this concept," and a "b" section, "The common understanding of time and the return to original time." Section "a" is divided into *alpha*, "Outline of Aristotle's treatise on time", 232–37, and *beta*, "Interpretive exposition of Aristotle's concept of time," 237–55.

49. Chapter 3, "Everywhere Now: Physical Time in Aristotle," *The Syntax of Time,* 87–105.

50. Ch. 10, 217b30. Translation mine from *The Syntax of Time*, Appendix 1, 153. All translations of Aristotle to follow are from that same appendix, though for better fit with Heidegger's discussion I change my translation of *to proteron kai husteron* there as "the beforehand/afterward" to "the earlier/later" here.

unproductive impasses. Several of these are discussed in the first lines of the chapter, followed by a very brief survey of earlier positions on the nature of time.

The first of the common sense perplexities is indeed mentioned in this opening sentence; namely, whether time is being or nonbeing. This, however, does not epitomize the several questions that Aristotle goes on to take up in the first part of chapter 10, and it is *not of programmatic interest* to him. He will later address and carefully formulate an explanation of what it means "to be in time" (*en chronô einai*), but whether time is being or nonbeing is not an issue for him, certainly not beside the question of settling its nature.

Heidegger opens his outline of the treatise by citing the same opening sentence, but he maintains that it "defines the inquiry."

> The first chapter, being first (Chapter 10), defines the inquiry, which moves in two directions. The first question is: *poteron tôn ontôn estin ê tôn mê ontôn*, does time belong among beings or non-beings? . . . The second question runs: *tis hê phusis autou*? (What is the nature, the essence of time?)[51]

Heidegger's misunderstanding of the treatise is evident right out of the gate. In a certain sense, the first chapter "defines the inquiry," but, to a great extent, it does so in a negative way. Heidegger thinks that whether time belongs among beings or nonbeings is a programmatic concern of Aristotle's. I argue that this is not the case. Even he admits,

> These two questions, about time's *mode of being* and its *essential nature,* receive proportionately unequal treatment. The first question is discussed in lesser detail; the positive answer is given only in the last chapter (14). The ensuing portions of the treatise are devoted to the investigation and discussion of the second question, What is time?

It would of course have been of great interest to Heidegger if Aristotle had taken up the question of time's "mode of being," but here Heidegger

---

51. GPP 330, BPP 232–33. Hofstadter transliterates the Greek, but does not mark for *eta* and *omega*, which I supply. He also does not italicize the foreign text, which I correct in the service of legibility.

himself tells us that, apart from some early lines of chapter 10 where it is discussed "in lesser detail," the topic that Aristotle's treatise addresses concerns the *nature* of time.

Of those lines, the "being" question receives only seven or eight, one of which makes the striking observation that "time does not seem to be put together out of Nows" (218a7), one of only two or three places in the treatise where Aristotle uses the plural *ta nun* to refer to an indefinite plurality. Elsewhere, the question is always whether Now is *one* or *two* (and it is two in a twofold way, touched on below). But another question takes up some twenty lines, and it anticipates issues that do figure in subsequent chapters, extensively, though not in Heidegger's outline. This is the question whether the Now, which appears to divide the past and future, is one and the same, or is always "other and other" (*allo kai allo*). In the midst of setting out this dilemma, Aristotle lays down a very important principle:

> For we may lay it down that it is impossible for the Nows to be neighbors of one another, any more than a point of a point. (218a18)

This is the first of many places where Aristotle signals his wariness at leaving himself vulnerable to Eleatic problems about continuity, and it is ominous that Heidegger doesn't seem to share, or perhaps, as we shall see, even to understand this concern.

As chapter 10 ends, having found both commonplace assumptions and predecessor opinions unfruitful, Aristotle makes a beginning of his own. He first establishes that time is not a motion, and then at the beginning of chapter 11, that it is not apart from motion. Hence it must be *tês kinêseôs ti* (something about motion) (219a10). This is a question for phenomenology. If time is something about motion, *what*? What, in the phenomena of motion, constitutes motion's timelikeness?

Heidegger did not attempt to answer this question with anything like phenomenological originality, because before he turned to Aristotle's treatise he already had his own answer: the countability of the Nows. As I will argue below, his way of arriving at a plurality of Nows does not explicate any argument in Aristotle's text. Yet he believes that making time a count of nows has a textual foundation: the formulation he cites as Aristotle's "definition of time."

I have been placing that formula in scare quotes, because there are two earlier passages that are candidates for "definitions" of time, both of which are phenomenologically richer than the one Heidegger cites, and both of which he ignores entirely. After his glance at predecessor statements about time toward the end of chapter 10, Aristotle opens his own inquiry, as we saw, with arguments to show that time is not motion. He gives two. Heidegger cites the first and outlines its role correctly.

> Now the change and motion of each thing is only *in* the thing itself which changes, or *where* the moving and changing thing itself happens to be; but time is alike both everywhere and with all things. (218b12)[52]

But the second argument, he ignores:

> Again, all change is faster and slower, but time is not; for the slow and fast are defined by time—fast is much movement in a short time, slow little in a long time; but time is not defined by time, neither by being a certain quantity of it nor a quality. (218b15)

Aristotle directs our attention to a specific aspect of phenomenal motion, the fact that among themselves, motions are faster and slower. The fast and slow are "defined by time" (*chronô hôristai*). Heidegger may well have seen this passage as empty semantics, but I have found that it is not.

Implicit in it is a specification of the *nature* of time: *time is that with respect to which we discriminate the faster and slower in motions. This* brings to view the dimension of nature, taken globally, that is most relevant to the study of time. I call this dimension *frame-space*. It arises from that comparability among concurrent motions by which we recognize that we can *count* faster ones with respect to slower ones. The framing of motion was the context in which time was originally designated "number of motion," by the old Pythagorean Archytas. This carried through Plato, *Timaeus* 37d, into Neoplatonism. Frame-space is

52. My translation and italics, ST 155. Heidegger cites it GPP 332, BPP 234–35.

a harmonic space; time-numbers are frequencies, counts of motions with respect to other motions, as in three of these against four of those.[53]

Insight into this original way in which time and number are associated is provided by a feature of the clock-face to which Heidegger devotes no attention, the *numbers of time*. Why are there twelve hours on the clock? The clock-face is a circle, and could perfectly well have seven or thirteen divisions. Why twelve? Because twelve has nice halves, thirds, and fourths. Sixty, the next number of time (seconds in a minute, minutes in an hour), is just a nicer twelve, divisible by halves, thirds, fourths, and fifths. The clock stands in for divisions of the rotation of the heaven of the stars, so 360, the number assigned to a complete revolution, is also a number of time, with nice halves, thirds, fourths, fifths, and sixths.

In the Pythagorean view, concurrent motions, most notably cyclic ones, tend to stabilize themselves in frame-space, first harmonically, and then in synchronicities and entrainments, which gives rise to the notion of number as an active power. Aristotle wants none of this, but insofar as chapter 14 takes its agenda from *Timaeus*, he can't get away from it. In chapter 11, however, he arrives at the formula that time is "number of motion" in a very carefully constructed argument of his own. Since Heidegger ignores the very core of this argument, there is no help for it but to summarize it myself.

The sample motions Aristotle considers in the treatise on time are all instances of traversal (*phora*). It does not at all follow that he reduces all other sorts of change or motion to change of place, but traversal enabled him to set out spatial magnitude as the backdrop for his argument.

> Now [*de*] since a thing moving is moved *out of* something *into* something, and all magnitude is continuous, motion corresponds to magnitude; for on account of the fact that the magnitude is continuous, the motion too is continuous; and through the motion, time. For how much the motion, just so much too does time ever seem to have happened. (219a11)

53. In musical notation, this is the format for what is called the "time signature." Modern notation shows both the rhythmic and harmonic features of music, but not its speed of succession, its *allo kai allo*. This can be suggested as a metronome setting, but that is extraneous to how musical notation shows time.

The strategic reason for this beginning will emerge shortly, but tactically, Aristotle has brought continuity into play via magnitude, then into motion which "corresponds to" (*akoleuthei*) magnitude, and then finally into time, for "however much" (*hosê*) there is of motion, "just so much" (*tououtos*) is there of time.

Aristotle then begins the argument that will indeed define time.

> Now then [*to dê* . . .]: the earlier/later is first of all in place; therein, however, in respect to *position* [*têi thesei*]. (219a15)

I am writing "the earlier/later" for *to proteron kai husteron* because they name an ordering distinction that applies across an entire expanse, like left/right, not a comparative distinction like before and after, which considers two positions at a time. The expanse here is the trajectory of the motion, say a baseball throw, taken as a *plurality of positions*. These are not yet regarded as sequential. As ordered, they comprise a series, but if succession (Aristotle says *allo kai allo*) is any kind of hallmark of the timelikeness of motion, then so far, everything timelike has been preemptively excluded from the formula "number of motion with regard to the earlier/later." If earlier/later is first of all in space (place), the formula reduces to "number of motion with regard to position in space," which says "number of local motion" or *phora* (traversal). If this is indeed a time-identifying statement, it is left to *number* to carry all the weight.

After a couple of lines in which earlier/later, like continuity, is tracked through the series magnitude//motion//time, Aristotle is ready for *horizmos*, definition. The first step is purely formal.

> We *recognize* [*gnôrizomen*] time when we define/identify [*horizômen*], the motion determining/horizoning [*horizontes*] the earlier/later. (219a23)

The verb *horizô* is the source of our word horizon. It means "to define" or "identify," its key sense being to mark out by boundary. In Aristotle, it is often appropriate to say "to horizon" in a phenomenological sense, since the function of a *horizmos* is to let the things defined appear in their whatness or essence. In the case of natural kinds, an important prescription is that there is no definition of individuals, not because individuals are not essence or primary being (*ousia*), but precisely because they are. If it is "tiger" that we wish to define, we can think of the Aristotelian procedure as akin to gradually narrowing the focus of something like a window, until only individual tigers appear in it: following a series like vertebrates, mammals, cats, tigers. Here, where time is concerned, we want to bring motion to appear specifically in its timelikeness. Aristotle tells us that we will do so by "horizoning the earlier/later." The earlier/later thus *cannot* be the defining feature of time. This is the very thing he has insured against by saying that it is first of all in place.

The analysis continues, touching first on the perceptual dimension of recognizing time:

> We then affirm time to have happened, when we take perception [*aisthêsin labômen*] of the earlier/later in the motion. (219a.24)

Again, this means we let the motion appear in the non-timelike plurality of positions in its trajectory. We meet with time when we go on to horizon the earlier/later *by the other and other*, and this is a *noetic*, not an aesthetic accomplishment.

But we define/identify/horizon by the other and other,

> grasping [*hupolabein*] them and something in between [*metaxu ti*] different to them;

> for when we apprehend [*noêsômen*] the extremes different from the middle and the Soul says the Nows two,

> the one earlier, the other later,

> then and this we affirm to be time.

> For what is defined/identified/horizoned by the Now seems to be time.

> And let this be laid down. (219a26–30)

What comes to light as time is the "something in between," is apprehending other and other as *spanned*. To the question, "Time is something about motion: What?" my answer is, the *spanning, framing,* and *scaling* of motion, where spanning is foundational for the other two.

What should we make of the curious phrase, "the soul says the nows two" (*duo epei hê psuchê ta nun*)? Are there two nows implied in the sheer incessancy Aristotle wants to convey with his *allo kai allo*? Why then does he say "Now" in the singular in the closing summary statement, "For what is defined/identified/horizoned by the Now seems to be time" (*to gar horizomenon tô nun chronos einai dokei*)? Here, finally, we are only five lines away from the *arithmos kinêseôs* formula: Is the soul "saying the nows two" an act of *counting,* to be continued to three, four, and so on?

That would be completely the wrong way to look for "number" in what I call the *logos* of time, its formula: "number of motion." It should be noted first that the definition of time (*horizmos*) that leads up to that *logos* involves an integration of the perceptual and the noetic. We are said to have "taken perception of" the earlier/later order. But we intellectually apprehend (*noêsômen*) the metaxy. For the unity of such an integration, one has to look to soul. The topic of soul comes up naturally, from within Aristotle's phenomenology.

The soul "says." The soul says the nows two. The soul "says the now in two," transitively, spanning motion. I think of it as opening a kind of window into motion, a window in which motions show themselves as numbersome, *among themselves in frame space*, in the comparability manifest in the faster and slower.

I have another reason for calling the dimension in which this comparability subsists "frame space." Our experience of motion is framed between motions too fast to be seen as moving, and too slow. The movement of the moon across the sky is too slow to perceive as moving, but glancing up at it from time to time makes evident that it is. Similarly the beating of a hummingbird's wings is too fast to resolve as movement. These limits are remarkably stable; no number of cups of coffee will help you follow the hummingbird's wingbeats, just as no meditative composure will let you see the moon moving. We readily assume the "too fast" and "too slow" to be physical properties of physical motions, yet time-lapse and time-dilation photography show that they can be coherently presented in other time-frames entirely. In time-lapse movies, for example, plants can be seen not just to move but to behave.

The limits on our living frame-space are conspicuously mind-dependent, or better, dependent on the soul. But they pertain to perceived physical motions.

The concrete way in which concurrent motions have number I call *scaling*. In the program of *The Syntax of Time*, I place Aristotle's "number of motion" within this essentially Pythagorean tradition of associating time with number. Apart from these few heuristic reflections, I will not replicate that analysis here. Scaling is at best only indirectly taken up in the treatise on time, for the reason that Aristotle's whole plan is to move away from time as *number* of motion to time as *measure* of motion, hence from time as plurality (*pleithos*) to time as a *magnitude* (*megathos*). This is the strategic reason for the assignment of earlier/later to magnitude. Since representing time as a measurable magnitude is a necessary first step toward analytic geometry and every sort of modern physical mechanics, it is understandable that modern readers are not only drawn to Aristotle's movement in that direction, but identify it as the essence of his contribution.

I have protracted the analysis of the spanning passage because it is the basis for the challenging statement Aristotle makes in chapter 14:

> And if nothing other than soul and the mind of soul were so natured as to number, time would be impossible, there being no soul—[54]

All but universally, commentators treat the phrase "soul and the mind of soul" (*psuchê kai psuchês nous*) as hendiadys or simple redundancy. I have argued that it is precisely in a psychical integration of *aisthêsis* and *noêsis* that motion has count or number, so that the passage in chapter 11 is marked as the antecedent for this claim in chapter 14, while the terms of this claim ("so natured as to number") confirm that in the passage in chapter 11, the "soul saying" pertains to number.

The challenge of the statement is to square it with Aristotle's familiar "realism." Certainly he is not claiming that time is an artifact of consciousness in any modern phenomenalist or idealist sense. The "substrate" (*ho pote on*) of time is motion, which is to say nature taken

---

54. *ei de mêden allo pephuken arithmein ê psuchê kai psuchêa nous, adunaton einai chronon psuchês mê ousês*, 223a 25.

globally (nature as "movable being"), and about this, Aristotle is dependably realist. On the other hand, time belongs to nature as its *phenomenon*, as its showing face. Time is something nature shows to the soul. It is the phenomenon of the phenomenal as such.[55]

Heidegger cites this passage from chapter 14 in *Being and Time*, near the end of §81, "Within-time-ness and the genesis of the ordinary conception of time." Just two paragraphs after his remark about how if one begins with time, there is no access in the reverse direction to temporality, he seems to allow for something like that after all.

> Although, proximally and for the most part, the ordinary experience of time is one that knows only 'world-time', it always gives it a *distinctive* relation to 'soul' and 'spirit', even if this is still a far cry from a philosophical inquiry oriented explicitly and primarily toward the 'subject'.[56]

The implication is that where that "*distinctive* relation" emerges (Heidegger's emphasis), it is possible to catch sight of the phenomenological basis of the ancient interpretations. Heidegger does not present the ordinary time-concept as illegitimate, but throughout the chapter is at pains to argue that it has a genuine foundation in temporality. "As evidence for this, he says "two characteristic passages will suffice," and he goes on to cite from Aristotle and Augustine. His exhibit from Aristotle is the claim in chapter 14:

> *ei de mêden allo pephuken arithmein ê psuchê kai psuchês nous, adunaton einai chronon psuchês mê ousês.* . . . (Left untranslated by Heidegger.)

> And if nothing other than soul and the mind of soul were so natured as to number, time would be impossible, there being no soul—[57]

---

55. Concluding sentence of *The Syntax of Time*, 151. Preparing for it is a major goal of the Aristotle chapter.

56. SZ 427, BT 479.

57. I leave off, as does Heidegger, the proviso that follows: "unless time is, like motion (if it turns out that motion can be without soul), just a 'this' which is being at the time (*ho pote ôn*)." Although that proviso complicates the question whether

How this observation by Aristotle is "characteristic" is unclear, since even in the more detailed exegesis of the treatise on time that Heidegger provides in *Basic Problems of Phenomenology*, he never directly addresses the passage. As we shall see shortly, it is certainly not prepared for by his account of now-time and counting the nows. In analytical circles, it is so unwelcome that it has been taken as evidence that the whole of chapter 14 is spurious.[58] In his footnote identifying the passage, Heidegger suggests we compare two of the three passages in chapter 11 that refer to the soul. These address subordinate moments in the argument that even though time is not a motion, it is not apart from motion. Neither ascribes any constitutive role for the soul in the phenomenon of time. The third mention of the soul in chapter 11, however, does, and this is the passage just discussed, to which Heidegger is entirely oblivious.

It is largely beside the point, however, to complain that Heidegger has overlooked or misunderstood this or that passage in Aristotle, because his derivation of time as ordinarily understood from temporality does not proceed as exegesis of the treatise on time at all. It reaches its own conclusion first, and then attempts to ascribe that to Aristotle by a forced interpretation of the number/count of motion "definition." Before considering whether that interpretation is correct or even coherent, let me summarize Heidegger's own derivation of time.

The story as it starts seems familiar and natural. It begins with reflection on the relationship between sight and light; specifically, between the circumspection (*Umsicht*) of Dasein's everyday concernful dealings, and sunlight as an essential constituent of the worldhood of the world. With respect to the sun, the world is *discovered* (or covered over). The time that everyday concern encounters in that discoveredness and comes to reckon with Heidegger calls "world-time" (*Weltzeit*).

In the varying manner in which sunlight occurs, Dasein is afforded Nows. These are not components of any theoretical construct, but are in each case a Now-*that*. It is dawn; now the cows are to be driven to pasture. It is evening; now they are to be brought in. Time is primally *worlded*, even ahead of its being reckoned with.

---

and how the being of soul is a condition for the possibility of time, it hardly softens it ("if it turns out that motion can be without soul").

58. Cf. *The Syntax of Time*, 89n 5.

Because world-time is brought about (*zeitigt*) by ecstatic temporality, the threefoldness of the ecstasies is reflected in it. Concern looks to *then* (*dann*, futural in German), when such-and-such is to be done, *on that former occasion* (*damals*), when such-and-such took place, and *now* that such-and-such is in order. Temporality is here the temporality of everydayness, which means that the then, formerly, and now have the unity of an *awaiting* that *retains* and *makes present*. Heidegger calls what is thus brought about by temporality *datability*. It is a foundational structure of world-time, not yet related to clocks or calendars.

In addition to their concreteness as modes of being-alongside, the "then when," "formerly when," and "now that" of datability all have the character of a "during," a spread. "Then when" will have its phases, its "beforehand this" and "beforehand that." Not only that, "then when" reveals its character of being "not yet now," so that from now to then there is also a during, and similarly with the "no longer now" of formerly. This expanse-character of world-time is called "spannedness," and Heidegger links it to an ecstatic "stretching along" of temporality itself.

Thus far only the being-alongside aspect of everydayness has been taken into account, but falling is also a mode of being-with-others. The third signature feature of world-time is "publicness" (*Öffentlichkeit*). Being-with-others is "under the same sky," and only on that basis can time-reckoning and the clock be approached.

> This dating of things in terms of the heavenly body which sheds forth light and warmth, and in terms of its distinctive 'places' in the sky, is a way of assigning time which can be done in our Being with one another 'under the same sky', and can be done for 'Everyman' at any time in the same way, so that within certain limits everyone is proximally agreed upon it.[59]

This seems like a simple observation it would be hard to take exception to, but in light of what will follow, I draw attention to something odd. Heidegger says that dating with the sun is "in terms of its distinctive 'places' in the sky." He means, for instance, dawn, from which he draws the rustic observation about the cows and the principle

---

59. SZ 413, BT 466.

that every Now is always a "now that." But the sun doesn't just occupy places in the sky, it is carried along a path by the equable circular turning of the sky. This opens into the question of what divisions should be marked in that path, which is where the twelve and sixty come in. The kind of situation Heidegger has in view involves synchronization, how two or more people come together someplace at the same time. For this the "peasant clock" suffices, stipulating a time in relation to pacing off the length of one's shadow. But again, this pertains to identifying a particular time in a public way, whereas what Heidegger wants to get to is *measuring* time. Two sentences after the above, he writes:

> This public dating, in which everyone assigns himself his time, is one which everyone can 'reckon' on simultaneously; it uses a publically available *measure*. This dating reckons with time in the sense of a *measuring of time*; and such measuring requires something by which time is to be measured—namely, a clock.

Something strange has happened here. Measuring pertains to expanse, to magnitude, and so far the sky has been considered only as featuring a variety of positions for the sun, and the publicness of time has come into reckoning only in regard to the problem of synchronizing. How does a reckoning with time, whose whole point is that everyone can do it simultaneously, use "a publically available *measure*"? And is *measuring* time what we do with a clock?

Obviously we can, though for that purpose it is handier to have a clock configured as a stopwatch or timer. But primarily, we use a clock to *tell time*, which is intrinsically related to synchronizing ourselves in world-time, and only indirectly to measuring time. Heidegger continues with an existential-temporal definition of "clock" that is peculiarly elusive.

> *This implies that along with the temporality of Dasein as thrown, abandoned to the 'world' and giving itself time, something like a 'clock' is also discovered—that is, something ready-to-hand which in its regular recurrence has become accessible in one's making-present awaitingly.* (All in italics.)

A clock is something ready-to-hand—a mechanical clock or a sundial. Even in the way that Dasein itself *is* the clock in the peasant clock, Dasein is ready-to-hand as a typical shape for casting shadows (italics Heidegger's). But the phrase "regular recurrence" introduces what is required of units for the measuring of time, though there is no evidence here that Heidegger is thinking either about the problem of what makes for convenient units in measuring expanses of time, or the related problem of how the expanse is given, since it is not a simultaneous whole. If instead it is the clock itself that regularly recurs, why that would be salient eludes me.

For all his attention to astronomical time-measuring and the need for mechanical clocks to be adjusted by it, I find only one brief passage in II, 6 where Heidegger adverts to the question of units or standards. He formulates correctly.

> Of course the number that we get by measuring can be read off [the clock face] immediately. But this implies that when a stretch is to be measured, we understand that our standard is, in a way, contained in it; that is, we determine the frequency of its *presence* in that stretch.[60]

That the numbers of time are *frequencies*, counts of intervals within intervals, leads to the spanning, framing, and scaling of motion, and to Aristotle as I understand him. But this passage is incidental to a point that for Heidegger looms much larger in the discussion of world-time, the Now.

> [W]hen we look at the clock and regulate ourselves *according to the time*, we are essentially *saying "now"*. Here the "now" has in each case already been understood and *interpreted* in its full structural content of datability, spannedness, publicness, and worldhood. This is so 'obvious' that we take no note of it whatsoever. Still less do we know anything about it explicitly.[61]

Regulating ourselves according to the time in everydayness, we avail ourselves of the clock with such transparency that the "saying now"

60. SZ 417, BT 469–70.
61. SZ 416, BT 469.

remains implicit only. But as he moves toward the derivation of Now-time, time as ordinarily understood, Heidegger considers how we look at a clock directly, for itself. This involves following the traveling pointer. As we do so, he says, we are tacitly repeating "now" and "now" and "now."

> Thus when *time is measured*, it is *made public* in such a way that it is encountered on each occasion and at any time for everyone as 'now and now and now'. This time which is 'universally' accessible in clocks is something that we come across as *a present-at-hand multiplicity of "nows"*, so to speak, though the measuring of time is not directed thematically toward time itself.[62]

When Heidegger uses the shorthand phrase "now-time," it is to indicate this representation of time as a present-at-hand multiplicity of "nows."

There is something ominous in the way that Heidegger talks about "nows." The "definition of time" he is on the way to appropriating from Aristotle speaks not of measure but of number, count. If time is a count of motion, the timelikeness of motion must involve plurality. But the only plurality that Heidegger has on the table is the "nows," which suggests that he plans to count them.

And that is just what he does. A few lines ahead of citing Aristotle's "definition of time," he writes:

> The existential-temporal meaning of [the use of clocks] turns out to be a making-present of the traveling pointer. By *following* the positions of the pointer in a way which makes present one *counts* them.

And shortly afterward, he summarizes,

> Time is what is 'counted'; that is to say, it is what is expressed and what we have in view, even if unthematically, when the *traveling* pointer (or the shadow) is made present. When one makes present that which is moved in its movement, one says 'now here, now here, and so on'. The "nows" are what get counted. And these show themselves 'in every "now" as "nows" which will 'forthwith be no-longer-now' and "nows"

62. SZ 417, BT 470.

which have 'just been not-yet-now'. The world-time which is 'sighted'
in this manner in the use of clocks, we call the *now-time*.[63]

Left entirely out of account here is that the traveling pointer, say a
second hand, traverses a *graduated* clockface. The "now here, now here,"
and so on are not randomly selected from the traveling in its *continuity*,
but rather from its reaching equally spaced marks that divide the minute
into sixty seconds. With some mechanical movements, the second hand
doesn't travel continuously at all, but leaps from one mark to the next.
Effaced entirely in Heidegger's reading of now-time from the clock is
the question of *units*. But only with reference to the units in use can any
counting become a measurement, and he holds that clocks measure
time. Counting nows alone won't do it.

The previous two citations are like bookends for Heidegger's
invocation of Aristotle. At the opening of this section, I drew attention
to a manipulation in Heidegger's translation of the "definition of time."
I present the text again:

> *touto gar estin ho chronos, arithmos kinêseôs kata to proteron kai husteron.*
> (Phys. IV, 11, 219b 1–2)

> This namely is time, what is counted in the movement encountered in
> the horizon of the earlier and later.

But the text does not say that time is what is counted, but that *time is
the count. Motion* is what is counted. Hence with respect to time, motion
must feature plurality. I have already explained how I understand that
to be possible, and will not revisit the issue. But there are two additional
problems here. First, what is "the movement" that is encountered; and
second, how is Heidegger understanding "the horizon of the earlier
and later"?

To the first: Heidegger is not referring to any particular sample
physical motion, or even to the whole ensemble of concurrent motions in
nature, but to a "motion" peculiar to the "nows." And he thinks that by
"the horizon of the earlier and later," Aristotle is identifying time, and

63. SZ 420–21, BT 473–74.

THE TEMPORAL PROBLEMATIC OF *BEING AND TIME* ‡ 53

doing so in a phenomenally appropriate way. In his extended interpretation of Aristotle in *Basic Problems of Phenomenology*, Heidegger initially says that this "seems to be impossible":

> "Earlier" and "later" are time-determinations. Aristotle says, time is what is counted in the motion we encounter in the horizon of time (earlier and later). But this simply means that time is something met within the horizon of time.

Heidegger thinks that Aristotle's formulation has this structure, but believes he can rescue it from elementary logical fallacy by claiming that the time named first is time as ordinarily understood, and the time in the "earlier and later" is original time, temporality.[64]

So he constructs a phenomenological exhibition to show that timelike continuity has a character of its own, unlike that of spatial continuity. It is often highly ingenious, but I shall not invest the labor of expounding it, because it goes wrong right from the start. Timelike continuity is met in the earlier/later, *to proteron kai husteron*, Heidegger wants to argue, so he cites Aristotle's opening statement about this phrase:

> In one place Aristotle says about *proteron* and *husteron*, *to de proteron kai husteron en topô proton estin* (219a14), "it is first of all in place, in the change and sequence of places."[65]

But this is exactly what Aristotle does *not* say. He says the earlier/later is first of all in place, and "therein, however, in respect to *position* [*têi thesei*]." Unexpectedly, perhaps, but for tactical and strategic reasons touched on above, Aristotle does *not* treat the earlier/later ordering distinction as pertaining to the change and sequence of places, but to the trajectory of a motion, taken as an *array of positions*.

So when Aristotle opens his passage on "horizoning" time, and asks us first to "take perception" of the earlier/later in the motion, this means to see it as an ordered expanse of *spatial magnitude*. To bring motion to life, so to speak, to restore its succession, Aristotle uses not earlier/later

64. BPP 240–41.
65. BPP 246.

but "other and other," *allo kai allo.* "Other and other" is not brought in here as a beginning of count, i.e., "one, two . . . ," but as a *two* that is a *one*, the span that opens into frame-space. "But we define/identify/horizon by the other and other, grasping [*hupolabein*] them and something in between [*metaxu ti*] different to them." The *in between* is time.

The Greek word *nun* itself is a sort of acronym for the thought here. N (*nu*) is a continuitive consonant. One can extend it like a vowel, "nnnnnnn . . . ," laying down a kind of *nu*-flux. But to *say NUN*, one needs a second *nu*, and *in between* (*metaxU*) an *upsilon*. The "soul says the nows two" in saying "Now" itself.

In my account, "soul saying Now" opens our intuition into the numbersomeness of motion. Heidegger takes away the Now of number, while trying to number/count the "nows" in a construct that is untenable.

I will close with one final reservation related to Heidegger's overlooking of units in his account of the use of clocks. He is given to making mathematically careless statements about continua as point-sets, independent of whether the continuum in question is spatial or timelike. An especially clear example occurs in his early lecture, "The Concept of Time in the Science of History," where his effort at mathematical rigor makes the problem all the more evident.

> In the equations of motion—$x = x(t)$, $y = y(t)$, and $z = z(t)$—time is presupposed as an independent variable that changes in a consistent way, i.e. flows uniformly from one point to another without any leaps. Time is like a simple linear series in which each point of time is differentiated by its current position as measured from its initial position. Since any given point in time differs from the preceding one only by being the succeeding one, it is possible to measure time and therefore motion.[66]

As an "independent variable," time "changes in a consistent way." This way of speaking is warranted by Newton, who says that it "flows equably." But "from one point to another" is worrisome, harboring the fallacy that becomes explicit when he writes, "Any given point in time differs from the preceding one." There is no barrier to speaking of "each

66. *Becoming Heidegger* 66.

point" in a continuum, so long as one keeps in mind that they are infinite. But no meaning whatever can be given to a "next" point, because between any two points there are infinitely many more. In modern transfinite number theory, one expresses this property by saying the points are "dense on the line." Taking the infinity that Aristotle resisted to be that of the rational numbers, which in the modern sense are countable (a one-to-one correspondence with the integers or "counting numbers" can be exhibited), they are still dense on the line, something he understood very well: "For we may lay it down that it is impossible for the Nows to be neighbors of one another, any more than a point of a point" (218a18).

The only way to make the mathematical assertion about t as an independent variable that Heidegger wants, is to say that it "varies in a timelike way." But that of course is the whole problem; what is timelike varying? Taking on "each" real value "in turn"? Such a statement would be completely incoherent. Mathematically, one may take "varying in a timelike way" to be a perfectly sound intuition. It just cannot be clarified by reference to the point set. Which is to say that it is a primitive intuition, is not philosophically helpful, and on the down side, is full of hazard.

TEMPORALITY AND ETERNITY

Let me now introduce how I will go about connecting the eternity of divine life with the temporal problematic of *Being and Time*. For reasons stated in the previous section, in working on *The Syntax of Time* I learned to make myself independent of Heidegger on time. Something similar may be necessary when it comes to eternity.

In *Being and Time*, Heidegger is mainly negative about eternity, his attitude well captured in his dismissal of "an eternal observer exempt from Dasein."[67] In his 1924 lecture to the theological faculty at Marburg, "On the Concept of Time," he is less combative, opening with a familiar reason why, on the topic of time, one should begin with eternity.

> If time finds its meaning in eternity, then it must be understood by starting from eternity. The starting point and direction of exploration are thereby mapped out in advance: from eternity to time. This way of

---

67. SZ 106, BT 140.

raising the question is in order, provided that such a starting point is available to us, i.e. provided we have an acquaintance and an adequate understanding of eternity at out disposal.[68]

As he goes on to argue, this amounts to claiming access to God, but access to God is faith, and philosophy renounces any claims to faith. "When the philosopher ask about time, he has resolved to *understand time from out of time.*" This becomes the default position of *Being and Time.*

There exists, however, another context in which the question of the "direction of exploration" between eternity and time arises, but which does not require faith and is properly philosophical. I refer to Plotinus's *On Eternity and Time*, wherein he stipulates that because eternity and time relate as paradigm and image, one can move between them in either direction.[69] Plotinus's own choice is to begin with eternity, not for reasons of its dignity or accessibility, but because thinking from that starting place comports with the origin and nature of time. After six chapters on eternity, early in the first chapter on time, he writes:

> So, then, we must go down now from eternity to the enquiry into time, and to time; for there our way led us upwards, but now we must come down in our discourse, not altogether, but in the way that time itself came down.[70]

My own thinking about eternity is deeply indebted to Plotinus, including my way of presenting Augustine's originality, but Plotinus is no use to us here. Heidegger is very uncomfortable with him. He taught a course on "Plotinus and Augustine" (SS 1921),[71] but regards Plotinus as an adverse influence. In the monograph expansion of *The Concept of Time*, he notes early on that "soul" and "mind" figure prominently in ancient research on time, and names "the two foundational treatises on

68. *Becoming Heidegger* 198.

69. Cf. III, 7, 1:17–25.

70. III, 7, 7: 8–11, trans. A. H. Armstrong

71. Topic as described by Heidegger in the 1922 Vita he sent to G. Misch, in *Becoming Heidegger* 108.

time that have been handed down to us, apart from the one by Plotinus."
As it turns out, they give the same passages from Aristotle and Augustine
that he uses in the same context in *Being and Time*—though there
Plotinus is simply discarded unmentioned.[72]

That is probably just as well. When he is forced by his own format, a
thumbnail sketch of the history of philosophical interpretations of time,
to mention *Peri aiônos kai chronou*, he translates the title "On the Aeon
and on Time," adding, "Aeon is a peculiar form intermediate between
eternity and time."[73] He is thinking of the medieval Latin concept of
aevum, which is certainly not what Plotinus means by *aiôn*, and
introduces a rabbit's hole of scholastic distinctions and complications that
we must definitely avoid.

There is however one positive remark on eternity in *Being and Time*,
which is useful for my purposes in this section. In the paragraph
immediately prior to the citations from Aristotle and Augustine,
Heidegger gives a summary restatement of the priority of the future in
ecstatic-horizonal temporality, and how that differs from the centrality
of the present and the leveled-off "now" in the ordinary conception of
time. To that paragraph he attaches a footnote that begins:

> The fact that the traditional conception of "eternity" as signifying the
> 'standing "now"' (*nunc stans*), has been drawn from the ordinary way
> of understanding time and has been defined with an orientation
> toward 'constant' presence-at-hand, does not need to be discussed in
> detail.

Once again, "traditional" here means Latin scholastic, and is
completely unrelated to my project. But having himself volunteered to
speak about eternity, Heidegger goes on to add a positive suggestion, and
from that I gain something of a foothold.

> If God's eternity can be 'construed' philosophically, then it can be
> understood only as a more primordial temporality which is 'infinite'.

72. CT 12, SZ 427, BT 479–80.
73. BPP 231.

Whether the way afforded by the *via negationis et eminentiae* is a possible one, remains to be seen.[74]

This at least puts eternity—and specifically the eternity of divine life—into the same sentence with temporality, opening for me a way into the topic of this section.

The theological *via* here mentioned is actually a compound one, joining two of three familiar medieval ways of argument to God that are governed by concern for divine transcendence. A first, the *via causalis* (causal way) argues from the creature on the basis of God as first cause. For Thomas Aquinas, the "existence" of God can be demonstrated in this way; for Heidegger of course it would mean presence-at-hand, and so be entirely unsuitable. The way of negation applies when a feature of the divine being so transcends that of the creature that one can only indicate it by negation of the created feature. If Dasein can be thought as creature, and *finite* temporality constitutes its being, then God's eternity, by negation, must be *infinite* temporality. The way of eminence identifies perfections in the creature whereby it is *capax deo*, capable of God or ordered to union with God, and ascribes them to God to an eminent degree. Here, the implication is that temporality is such a feature, so that the divine eternity has to be a *more primordial* temporality.

There are complications with either side of this suggestion. First, it is difficult enough to get readers of *Being and Time* to appreciate that the "finitude" of finite temporality is an intrinsic, structural aspect of its unity, not a limitation imposed from outside, and nothing at all like saying that the human lifespan is inevitably a limited length of time. To say that eternity is infinite worsens the risk of such a misunderstanding, because eternity (*aeternitas*) itself is too readily misconstrued as endless time (*sempiternitas*). As for the notion of a "more primordial" temporality, this too has its problems, since temporality is already "primordial time," the horizon for the projection of the meaning of being in any case of it.

At root, all these ways unfold within a theological systematics that is fundamentally *Christological* in structure, treating first of God and the creature as from God, second of the creature as ordered to God and returning to God, then third, of Christ the mediator. In this project I am

74. SZ 427n, BT 499n xiii

espousing a *trinitarian* fundamental theology, specifically an Augustinian one, which sets as its key philosophical challenge not the metaphysical problem of transcendent creator and finite creature, but a very particular *disclosure* problematic. At issue is human authenticity as *image of God* (*imago dei*), specifically an image of divine *trinity*—Father and Son in one Spirit.

In Greek Christian theology prior to Augustine, "image of God" meant specifically the Son alone, and being created "in the image of God" (Genesis 1:26) meant being created in the Son, in the divine Logos. Likewise, being restored to the image of God meant being restored to union with the Logos. The creator is the Father, and the begetting of the divine Logos is a preliminary moment in the creation of the world. Reflection on the Father and the Son remains caught up with the inherently metaphysical doctrine of creation to such a degree that a fully trinitarian account of divine life is largely thwarted before Augustine. Emblematic of this is the original Nicene Creed (325), in which the article on the Spirit is just a stub: ". . . and [we believe] in the Holy Spirit."

For Augustine in *On Trinity*, God the creator is now the trinity, acting as one, on the principle that acts of God "to the outside" (*ad extra*) are indivisible. Hence from creation as such, nothing about the inner divine life, Father and Son in the unity of the Spirit, is evident. The theological context for the trinity is no longer the doctrine of creation but the doctrine of *revelation* (New Testament and tradition), and because authentic human being is an image of the trinity, *human being becomes a dimension of revelation as well.*

These brief anticipations of chapter 2, "The Temporality of Trinity in Augustine" allow me to indicate, in a formal way, the line of thought that connects *On Trinity* to *Being and Time*. Augustine argues that because image of God is what we are, our very mode of being creatures, it cannot be destroyed by original sin, but only veiled or effaced. It is constituted at the highest summit of the "inner human," "between which and God *nulla natura interposuit* (no nature interposes)." But first of all and mostly, we live according to the "outer human," captivated by the affairs of embodied life, drawn away from the "more inward way" that leads to the true self, "within which is God." When the desire for knowledge of God is awakened by faith, however, we discover in ourselves an "unknown mind," a mind we know, in that we do not know it, but which *calls to us*. The program of *On Trinity* follows that call, from the outer human to the inner human, and then, within the inner human, from our concern for the good and the true in time to true wisdom, which is eternal. At each level, Augustine conducts a phenomenological reflection that is schematized triadically: *memoria, intelligentia, voluntas* (memory, understanding, will *or* freedom). At the most outward level of the outer human, where there is only a vestige of the image of God, the phenomenology considers the unity of retention, attention, and intention in sense experience. In a pattern repeated in the whole inward/upward way, the third term is not only what unifies the first two, but it is also *higher* than them, already participating in the next level. Therefore the triadic schema is not merely statically reflected at each level, but is the dynamic principle of the ascent itself.

As an exercise in philosophical anthropology, the ascent culminates in the self-constitution of inwardness itself, mind as self-memory, begetting self-understanding, in the unity of self-love. I claim that the memory/understanding/love triad is a *temporal* triad, in the sense of *Being and Time*. In calling itself back to itself from its lostness in the everyday, inwardness is active as authentic will, so that the futural term takes the lead, which corresponds to the role of the Holy Spirit in revelation.

2. The Temporality of Trinity in Augustine

THE WORD "TRINITY" is simply Latin for "triad." The title of Augustine's treatise on the topic is "on triad" (*de trinitate*). He does not capitalize *trinitas*, and if he needs to be understood as speaking of God, he has to stipulate *trinitas quae deus est*. Much of the philosophical work in this treatise, taking place in books VIII through XIV of the fifteen, is concerned with a trinity in human being. As alive in this trinity, human being is the *imago dei*, image of God, and it was Augustine's historic innovation to insist that being created in the image of God (Genesis 1:26) included reflecting the divine trinity.

In the Greek world prior to Augustine, the common view was that the phrase "image of God" designated directly the Son, the *logos*, "the image of the invisible God and the firstborn of all creation" (Colossians 1:15). Being created "in the image" meant being created in the *logos*, being *logikos* (rational). Human fallenness was interpreted as defection from the *logos*, and in that sense a veiling of the divine image (i.e., of the Son). Restoration of the image of God in human being involved the disclosure of Christ, the Son, through whom alone vision of the Father is possible.

I leave this account terse and schematic in order to indicate, equally schematically for now, the scope of Augustine's new, trinitarian account of *imago dei*. Restoring the human image amounts to a disclosure of the divine trinity, Father and Son in one Spirit. Essential to Augustine's approach is his conviction that even in human fallenness, the image of God is not completely effaced, but merely veiled. There remain vestiges, effigies susceptible to philosophical discovery. These share the structure of what is ordinarily called a "psychological" trinity, *memoria, intelligentia, voluntas*: memory, understanding, will. To call these "psychological" is misleading. In a general sense, this triad does reside "in the soul," but more properly, it constitutes the structure of *mens* (mind), *mens animi* (the mind of the soul).[1]

In this chapter I will show that Augustine's philosophical procedure is phenomenological, and, more specifically, that it amounts to a discovery and interpretation of ecstatic-horizonal temporality. Like Heidegger's procedure in *Being and Time*, it insists on beginning with and remaining grounded in everydayness (since falling itself is one of the ecstasies), while nonetheless seeking disclosure of human being in its authenticity. I will compare the methodologies of the respective phenomenologies later in this chapter.

First, however, I want to place the particular schema Augustine supposes for trinity within the context of triads prominent in his own historical context. Section 1 will introduce the "noetic triad," a "horizontal" triad that emerges in Plotinus, and is very different from the "vertical" hypostatic series with which Plotinus is most closely associated, the One, *Nous*, and *Psychê*. Augustine becomes aware of it indirectly, through Marius Victorinus, translator of the "Platonic books" that Augustine read.

Augustine's sense that something ecstatic needs to be sought in time is rooted in his appropriation of Plotinus's *On Eternity and Time* (*Ennead* III, 7), above all in Plotinus's registration of eternity as something intensive about time, not something extensive. This relationship will be summarized in a section to follow.

The ecstatic temporal horizon prominent in Neoplatonism is that of the present. Augustine's originality comes from his uniquely intense experience of ecstatic having been, of the past. In the next section I will argue that a foundational role for memory is first discernable in the early treatise *On Music*, then becomes programmatic and explicit in *Confessions*.

1. Augustine translates Greek *nous* as *mens*, and so, with complications generated by the fact that for Greek *psychê* he has in Latin both *anima* and *animus*, he distinguishes mind from soul as Plotinus does. Plotinus's usage is conformable to that of Aristotle *On Soul*. "Soul" pertains to the general ontology of the *zôon* (the living being), *soma* and *psychê* in hylomorphic unity. "Mind" (*nous*), is a specific power of soul, directed to the intelligible, just as perception (*aisthêsis* is directed to the sensible. How these distinctions function in *de trinitate* is detailed below.

Comparison of temporal interpretation in Heidegger and Augustine begins in two final sections, both of which are entitled "Temporal Interpretation and the *imago dei*," the first being methodological, the second phenomenological. This prepares for direct engagement with the theology of revelation in the New Testament in Chapter 3.

THE NOETIC TRIAD IN PLOTINUS, MARIUS VICTORINUS, AND AUGUSTINE

Looking for triads in pre-Augustinian Neoplatonism one can come too quickly upon Plotinus. If one adopts the convention of referring to the One, Mind, and Soul as "hypostases" (Plotinus himself does not), then there are decidedly three of them. So perhaps in some sense they make a triad.

But not a triad like the one in view in the orthodox summation of the doctrine of divine trinity as *mia ousia*, *treis hupostaseis*, one essence (Latin "substance"), three hypostases (Latin "persons"). The term hypostasis entered trinitarian theology mainly because of its vagueness. It is not a technical term in Aristotle or Plato. Augustine knows but prefers to avoid Latin "persons," finding it insufficiently vague. These two contexts for referring to a triad of hypostases must not be confused.

The triad that does provide philosophical context for Augustine's trinity is the noetic triad, *on, zôê, nous* (being, life, mind). Plotinus addresses it most directly in an enigmatic passage.

> If being (*to einai*) is sought, it is to be sought especially in what is most Being; and if wholly knowing (*to noein holôs*), then in what is most Nous; and so too of Life itself.
>
> So if one needs to take primal Being as being first, and then Nous, and then the Living being (for this already seems to contain all things), then Nous is second (for it is an activity of essence).[2]

Here Plotinus imposes a different seriality upon the three terms than what later became the conventional order, *on, zôê, nous*. When cited in that order, discussion quickly emphasizes that Being/Nous is a kind of dyad, and that Life is the overarching and unifying factor, the "third

---

2. VI 6 [34], 8, lines 15–22, my translation.

term" (though mentioned second) and the one most directly communicated to Nous from the transcendent One.

Why does Plotinus need to take Being first, and directly affirm that Nous is second? This takes us to the question of derivation in Plotinus, especially in the direction of higher to lower. At one time this was characterized as "emanation," but this is at best half true. In speaking of the derivation of Nous from the One, Plotinus quite formally puts in play both *proodos* (emanation) and *epistrophê* (turning back, return). Here is an especially seminal passage.

> The One, perfect because It seeks nothing, has nothing, and needs nothing overflows, as it were, and Its superabundance makes something other than itself. This, when it has come into being, turns back upon the One and is filled, and so becomes its contemplator, Nous. Its halt and turning back toward the One constitutes Being, its gaze upon the One, Nous. Since it halts and turns toward the One that it may see, it becomes at once Nous and Being.[3]

Notice that the productive moment in this derivation is the return. It is a moment of self-collection or self-gathering. "Its halt and turning back toward the One constitutes Being." Prior to this moment, we were dealing only with the One, specifically its overflow. Now, we are in the "Second One," Nous. This Second One is first Being, then "its gaze upon the One [constitutes] Nous." Again and again, Plotinus stresses the unity of Mind and Being, in one such context (III 8, 9 citing with approval what we call fragment 3 of the Poem of Parmenides:

> For it is the same to think as well as to be (*to gar auto noein estin te kai einai*).

Even in the extremity of their unity, mind and being are a dyad for Plotinus, and in this he detects the necessity that they arise from a transcendent and absolute One, "beyond mind and being." Hence the unifying third term, "life," is a gift of the One, the mark of its proximity. Life, like Beauty, is a term Plotinus is tempted to apply to the One, just

---

3. V 2 [11], 1, trans. A. H. Armstrong, *Plotinus*. New York, 1962, 51.

as he comfortably calls it the Good. But strictly speaking, Life and Beauty belong to the Second One, not by way of denying them to the First, but as clearest signs of their having such an origin. (Indeed, against the gnostics, Plotinus accords Life and Beauty even to the Third One, nature and Soul.)

I have called the noetic triad "horizontal" in order to distinguish it schematically from the clear verticality of the one, two, three, the hierarchical series in Plotinus. It is a structure within "two," the second. As I can show from Augustine, the noetic triad is "horizontal" in a sense that includes a role for horizons, but for now I use it in a merely formal way, to distinguish it from the vertical, the order of derivation among One, Mind, and Soul.

There later emerged in Iamblichus an account of derivation itself that is vertical and triadic. This account was initially driven by the problem of participation, which in Plotinian terms becomes the problem of the derivation of Soul from Nous. Plotinus in On Eternity and Time directly addresses the verticality of this relationship when he says, of the transition from eternity to time:

> So, then, we must go down from eternity to the inquiry into time, and to time, for there our way led us upwards, but now we must come down in our discourse, not altogether, but in the way in which time came down. (III 7, 7; trans. Armstrong)

As I will show at length in the section to follow, time "came down" in such a way as to remain in contact with eternity. "Eternity and time" in Plotinus is one topic, not two. As Iamblichus noticed, their belonging together is the engine, so to speak, of participation. As an analytical tool for relations between levels in the overall systematic series, he developed a triadic "schema of participation." In this formalism, one distinguishes among three different states of any hypostasis or element in the derivational series:

i. that factor unparticipated (*amethektos*), "in itself," absolute;

ii. that factor participated (*metechomenos*), which involves a self-disposition and action by the factor, not a reaction to what participates in it; and

iii. that factor as participant (*kata methexin, en tois metechousi, en schesei*), that is, as enacted in the derived hypostasis and now its action, no longer that of the higher hypostasis.

In later Neoplatonism, notably in Proclus, this schema reacted back upon the hypostatic series itself, generating additional layers. Iamblichus took the lead in such ramification, introducing the eccentric postulate of an Unparticipated One, higher than the Plotinian One, which, because it was a participated one (*Nous* its participant), became for Iamblichus a second.

This move by Iamblichus has much to do with the widespread view that the systematic complications of late Neoplatonism are groundless speculation, artifacts of pure formalism. But if I am right that the most proper context for application of the schema of participation is Platonic participation itself, the relation between the sensible and the intelligible, then Plotinus's thesis that this relationship comes about in the derivation of time from eternity gives access to a phenomenological ground. At a minimum, the schema of participation explains why Iamblichus finds in Plotinus a distinction between an intellectual and a sensible time. Intellectual time is participated time, sensible time the participant. I will put this account to work in the next section.

After this brief indication of the philosophical issues embedded in the "vertical" aspect of the Plotinian system, I return to the "horizontal," and specifically to the noetic triad. Here, I argue that the philosophical issue is *mediation* within the *structure of self-constitution*. In what I said above about the emergence of Nous as a "halt" and "turn" within the overflow of the One, I stressed that this amounts to a self-collection, a self-gathering. "Self" itself, the selfsame (*to auto*), is "Mind as well as Being" (Parmenides), and for Plotinus this "as well as" (*te kai*) unfolds within a unity for which Life is the medium. The living belonging together of Mind and Being is the Second One. And it is divine life.

Plotinus consistently means the Being One, Nous, by the expression *ho theos* (God). The One beyond mind and being is not God. Even when, against the grain of his typical use of the neuter, impersonal pronoun "it" for the One, he employs a personal pronoun like "he"/"him"/"his," Plotinus never intends to identify the One with God, much less a personal God. It is very clear that Augustine's trinity unfolds on the level of the Being One; God is eternal true substance. For him, there is no supervening unity beyond that of the divine trinity itself. He is not at all drawn to the notion that there is a kind of theological "fourth," a Godhead beyond the trinity of Father, Son, and Spirit, a theme that emerged in later apophatic theology (pseudo-Dionysius, *The Cloud of Unknowing*, Meister Eckhart). Philosophically, that tradition reflects Plotinus more completely than Augustine does. Theologically, it begins from the premise that the trinity is God *as revealed*, coupled with dissatisfaction that this can be identified with divine life itself, in its own originality. Augustine has his own way of thematizing the aseity of God, but it does not involve a deeper unity than the trinity. His trinity is self-constituting unity, horizontal in the same way as the noetic triad.

Situated in a certain way between Plotinus and Augustine, Marius Victorinus resorts to the noetic triad expressly for its horizontal pattern, as distinct from the catastrophic "verticality" of Arianism, which models the Father and the Son on the Neoplatonic One and Nous, making the Son less than the Father. That the Son is derived from the Father is inescapable, because it is scriptural.[4] But Victorinus models his trinity on the horizontal derivational moment within the noetic dyad, a first engendering a second, the third serving as medium.

I find it fascinating that Victorinus cites the noetic triad as *esse, vivere, intelligere* (being, life, mind), thus furnishing evidence that this was the conventional order, and yet he interprets them as though they were serial in Plotinus's order (being, mind, life), though he does not otherwise follow Plotinus at all. For Plotinus, Being and Nous are the dyad, and Life the mediator. Victorinus thinks that *esse* and *vivere* make a pair, and that *intelligere* is the mediating third.

Compressed, his argument is as follows. Being is a moment of potentiality, not actuality. Of course it is potency, power, not mere possibility devoid of its own act. But it is not by itself the divine creative principle. Being must become doing, and only living being can "do" anything. In the Prologue to the Gospel of John, God-in-action is the Logos, and this Logos is "life" and the "light of men." God must "be,"

---

4. E.g., "Truly, truly, I say to you the Son can do nothing of his own accord, but only what he sees the Father doing; for whatever he does, that the Son does also." John 5:19 (RSV).

therefore, in such a way that life in action is already implicated in that being, and implicated not just as anticipation but in enactment.

Hence the aboriginal divine "substance" (*ousia*) is, as a matter of self-constitution and structure, eternally in action. As the primordial "to be" that harbors life as power, God is Father. As the living instrumentality that eternally declares and manifests the divine potency, God is Logos and Son. Both being and living address the divine substance, first in regard to its outgoing procession, its self-constitution as creative and salvific action. But within the divine substance, being and living are not just action but *intelligere*, contemplation, contemplative self-knowing. This is not super-added to being and life, but is the medium of their very distinction, though now in the mode of inwardness, not procession. This is the Spirit, third as a completing moment that brings us back to the first and hence itself designates the substance of God. The gospel statement that "God is Spirit" (John 4:24) refers to the one divine substance. As Augustine will later argue, it is appropriate that the Holy Spirit be named from that in which Father and Son are one.

Victorinus is not dependent on Plotinus in a literary sense. He has his own philosophical position, developed in conversation with doctrine and scripture. But he has clearly worked within the formalism of the noetic triad, especially its status as a horizontal structure internal to eternal true substance. A similar relationship obtains between Augustine and Victorinus. There is evidence that Augustine is aware of Victorinus as a theologian in his own right, and not just as the translator of Plotinus and Porphyry. He does not, however, replicate the philosophical explication Victorinus gives to the noetic triad in interpreting divine trinity. Augustine's triadic schema *memoria, intelligentia, voluntas* cannot be squared with either the Plotinian *on, nous, zôê,* or with Victorinus's *esse, vivere, intelligere,* because whatever one does about the order of the second and third terms, to make "memory" the first term is altogether original to Augustine. Where Augustine may in fact be spurred on by Victorinus is in the thesis that human noetic life is an image of the noetic triad.

Here Augustine found an opening for following intentional analysis of his own noetic life all the way to an unveiling of the image of divine trinity. His trinity follows the schema of the noetic triad not pedantically, but in direct phenomenological reflection on the truth of it. The phenomenology is grounded in an ecstatic understanding of memory,

memory as ecstatic having been, the foundational moment of inwardness or consciousness. I will sketch the building of that foundation in a later section of this chapter.

Before he could enter this whole new world, however, Augustine needed already to have encountered one of the ecstasies of ecstatic-horizonal temporality, that of ecstatic presence. He met with this in Plotinus's account of eternity and time.

ETERNITY AND TIME IN PLOTINUS AND AUGUSTINE

I said above that eternity and time make one topic, not two. I mean this in the original sense of the term "topic," which refers to a *topos* (place), a determinative place in a text. Plotinus's treatise *On Eternity and Time* is an extended meditation on a particular Platonic *topos*, *Timaeus* 37d:

> . . . simultaneously with setting in order the heaven, of eternity abiding in one, he (the father of this All) made an image of eternity moving according to number, this being what we have called time. (final lines of the passage, my translation)

At this point in the story, Soul has been built out of a musical scale construction treated as a flat expanse. Torn in two along its length, the resulting strips are connected into counter-rotating circles and set all through the body of, and enveloping the whole of, the corporeal heaven. Motion and life are everywhere, and yet in the story line there is still no time. In the lead-in to our passage, which begins at 37c, the reason for this delay is given: time comes in to make this heaven a *still better* likeness of its everlasting (*aïdion*) paradigm.

> Contemplating (*enoêsen*) that it moves (*kinêthen*) and lives (*zôn*), become a keepsake (*agalma*, thing of joy) of the everlasting gods, the engendering father wondered as well, and he contrived to make it a still better likeness for its paradigm. Now this is an everlasting living being (*zôon aïdion on*). He took on the task of making this All (*tode to pan*) like that as much as he could. But the nature of the living being happens to be eternal (*aiônios*), and it was not possible to attach this entirely to what is generated. So he planned to make a sort of mobile image of eternity, and . . . . (as above) (37c–d, my translation)

To read this with Plotinus, it is essential to preserve the distinction between "everlasting" (*aïdios*) and "eternal" (*aiônios*), something not all English translations attempt. Plotinus specifically notes that "we call the whole cosmos There" both *aiônion* and *aïdion*, eternal and everlasting, and he asks, "What is everlastingness? (*ti hê aïdiotês*)" (III 7, 3).

The heaven is everlasting for Plotinus in exactly the same way it is for Aristotle in *Metaphysics* (Lambda, 6): it has no beginning and no end, but endures throughout all time. In the translation "everlasting," the "lasting" needs to be heard. Aristotle also directly asserts that time is without beginning or end, but Plotinus exploits an artifact of the "likely story" Plato has Timaeus tell, to ask how time came to be at all—not in the sense of a timelike beginning, but rather as having placement in the order of natures or principles of life. The father and maker (himself a narrative artifact) undertook to make this All as much like its paradigm as he could, but confronted there a recalcitrant nature, eternity. "It was not possible to attach this entirely to what is generated."

By saying that an eternal nature could not be "attached" to what comes to be *entirely*, Plato leaves the implication that an eternal nature *can* be attached to sensible becoming *in some sense* or *to some degree*. This section will spell out the temporalities involved in this situation. They all cluster around the proposition that the eternal is *present*, and "necessarily there is no 'was' nor 'will be' about it" (*ex anangkês oute to ên hexei peri auto, . . . oute to estai*) (III 7, 3: 30–32). I begin by drawing out the implications for Plotinus of the paradigm/image relation itself.

Toward the end of the opening chapter in *On Eternity and Time*, after duly noting the value of studying the opinions of others, Plotinus shifts his attention to how it might be possible that "for us too there could be direct understanding (*sunesis*, "with-ing") of these things." He continues:

> And first is to inquire about eternity, what sort of thing those who hold it to be other than time consider it to be. For when that which holds the position of paradigm is known, it may become clear how it is with its image, which time is said to be. But if before contemplating eternity, someone should picture (*phantasthaeiê*) what time is, it would be possible for him, too, to go from this world to the other by recollection, and contemplate that of which time is a likeness, if time really is a likeness of eternity. (III 7, 1: 17–24, my translation)

He introduces a question of philosophical method at a very high level. Given that they make one topic, there are two possible orders in which the paradigm and image could be considered. If one can begin from the paradigm eternity as known (*gnôsthentos*), it may come clear (*saphes genoito*) how it stands with (*hestôtos*) the image, time. On the other hand, given what might be argued as the superior availability of insight into time, perhaps it is more attractive to begin there and then move by recollection into contemplation of eternity. Both procedures are available.

One might suppose that the second path, the one from time to eternity, would be the more likely to have importance for phenomenology. The phrase Plotinus uses to designate the philosophical accomplishment required to begin from time is "form-a-picture-in-the-mind of how time is" (*ton chronon hôs esti phantastheiê*). The verb, a subjunctive, is rare and formal; it could be a neologism, constructed by making a verb from *phantasia* (imagination), giving it the sense of a constructive activity. Such an idea is available in Aristotle, who places *phantasia* between *aisthêsis* and *nous*, imagination between perception and intellect/mind in book III *On the Soul*. It is messy, but one might even ask about the relation in Aristotle between *phantasia* and *ta phainomena*, imagination and the phenomenal. All this sounds promising for phenomenology.

Plotinus, however, choses the other path, the first path. He begins with eternity, then "goes down" to time. This does not amount to a forgoing of phenomenology, but leads directly to what is most characteristic about time from a phenomenological point of view. In the order of his own exposition, he takes the path from eternity to time because in the transcendental logic of his position, this is the order of derivation. But, as he makes clear in the transitional seventh chapter, the direction of *phenomenological* insight is from time to eternity.

> What it means to be in time and what it means to be in eternity may become known to us *when we have discovered time* (*heurethentos tou chronou*).[5]

---

5. III 7, 7: 6–8, trans. A. H. Armstrong, emphasis added. Unless otherwise stated, all citations will be from Armstrong's translation.

Although by this point in the treatise both the logical structure of eternity (chapters 2–4) and its nature (chapters 5–6) have been fully developed, "what it means to be 'in' eternity" (*pôs en aiôna estin einai*) remains as undetermined as to be "in" time. For both of these, surprisingly, the account of time is the heuristic. The reason for this is that *time itself reaches from eternity to time.* Though it has "come down" from eternity, it has not done so "altogether":

> So, then, we must go down from eternity to the enquiry into time, and to time; for there our way led us upwards, but now we must come down in our discourse, not altogether, but in the way in which time came down.[6]

The way in which discovery of the timelike throws light on eternity is not by referral upwards, so to speak, but through exposure of the "eternal downwards," the descending movement of the soul in which time originates.

This is a *temporal ecstasis*, articulating the horizonal schema of the ecstatic present. Heidegger connects it with falling, one of the constitutive items of the care-structure. Comparison of Heidegger's and Augustine's respective phenomenologies of falling will become central to the discussion later in this chapter, including their nearly identical ways of addressing "everydayness." Here, I need first to show how the "horizonal schema" of ecstatic-temporal presence is reflected in Plotinus's account of time as image of eternity.

Until now, I have carefully not spoken of temporality or the temporal in this section, except in a passing and promissory way, but have used and will continue to use the term "timelike," saying for example that what is everlasting has no timelike beginning or end. Without clarity about how Plotinus identifies time and the timelike, there is no access at all to the temporal structure of his position, much less to what marks it as ecstatic. If time is image and eternity is paradigm, then far from being "timeless," eternity is *paradigmatically timelike.*

After chapters on eternity (III 7, 2–6), and a critical review of predecessors' opinions on time (7–10), Plotinus's positive account of time

---

6. III 7, 7: 8–11.

begins in chapter 11, which continues and exploits Plato's productive use of *mythos* (narrative) in *Timaeus*. A complete presentation of Plotinus's phenomenology of time by way of interpretation of this chapter is out of reach here. On the dramatic level alone, it is a very complex composition. I will bring forward here some of the summary formulations I developed in the Plotinus chapter of *The Syntax of Time*,[7] attaching them to the text in a more limited way.

What is often referred to as Plotinus's "definition of time" is presented as a question, though it arrives at a point in the chapter where the formulation is clearly meant to have some kind of canonical force.

> So if someone were to say time to be the life of soul (*psychês . . . zôên*) in a movement of transition (*en kinêsei metabatikê*) from one way-of-life to another (*ex allou eis allon bion*), would this say something sensible (*dokoi ti legein*)? (III 7, 11:43–45, my translation)

One wants to say "yes," but there is a serious semantic problem here. How is one to differentiate between *zôê* and *bios*, both of which can be translated "life"? When I began trying to read this treatise from a phenomenological point of view in the late 70s, there was consensus that *zôê* meant "life" in the sense of a principle of living, something belonging to a nature. But about *bios*, where the transition from one of them to another belongs to the identity of time, I found only confusion. I finally decided that it derived from pervasive misidentification of the *phenomenon* of time itself.

In chapter 1, I mentioned Aristotle's observation that while time is not motion, it has to be *something about* motion. In Newton, Locke, and Hume, that something is presumed to be *succession*. Each of the most authoritative scholars I could read on III 7[8] assumed that the two *bioi* (lives) here must be successive much like stations in a lifetime: my college life, my early teaching life, and so on. This can be generalized, though with some artificiality, into positions along a time line. The presumption

---

7. Chapter 2, "Time and the Soul in Plotinus," ST 55–86.

8. J. F. Callahan, *Four Views of Time in Ancient Philosophy*, 1948; Hans Jonas, *Gnosis und Spätantiker Geist, Teil II*, 1966; Werner Beierwaltes, *Denken des Einen*, 1985.

was that with respect to time, the directionality of the life of soul was decidedly *horizontal*.

I found this to be massively untenable. I choose to translate *bios* in this context as "way of life," in order to accommodate the two that Plotinus specifically identifies. One is eternity, where life (*zôê*) is contemplative mind, intellect (*nous*). The other is time, where life is sensible motion and perception. The dimension in which the transition takes place is vertical, specifically the verticality of the schema of participation.

Undeniably, one these ways of life, sensible motion, involves succession, which I agree is horizontal. But time has both vertical and horizontal aspects. Vertically, time arises in the transition from eternity *into time*. Time moves into time? This is quite deliberately what Plotinus means. *Time is a perpetual "downward" arrival into itself*, into its own way of spanning sensible motion horizontally. Time is two-dimensional.

In the vertical dimension, time enacts soul's capacity to render intelligible beings participable by sensible motion. The schema of participation applied to the soul in this essentially cosmogonic context answers Aristotle's challenge: tell me how "participation" *works*.

In the horizontal dimension, time opens itself into *diastasis* (span *or* spread) across sensible motion. *Diastasis* is the reverse of *ekstasis*, standing out or away. *Diastasis* is standing through, but also standing across. What soul stands across is the successive phases of sensible motion. Without this spanning by soul, Plotinus teaches, successive phases would have no *order (taxis)*.[9]

In their Greek, Aristotle and Plotinus express the order in succession in importantly different ways. Aristotle evokes succession with the phase *allo kai allo*, other and other. What he wants to bring out about succession is its sheer incessancy. Plotinus mocks such a view of succession with the illustration "now Socrates, now a horse," appearances devoid of any intentional unity. Plotinus's phrase is *tode meta tode*, this *after* that, finally this *for the sake of* that. This points in the direction of *order* and an *ordering power*.

Order, *taxis*, is named from *tassô, tattein* (order [transitive]; put in order, arrange [frequently in a military context]). *Taxis* differs from *thesis*, mere position. The order in sensible motion results from soul, the

---

9. For Plotinus these are more likely to be *logoi* than the usual Platonic *eidê*.

living power that produces nature or embodied sensible being in the first place. "For we hold," Plotinus writes, "that time has its existence in the activity of soul and derives from it."[10] In the great treatise *On Difficulties about the Soul*, divided by Porphyry into three tractates with that title, IV 3 [27], IV 4 [28], and IV 5 [29], he confronts logical problems raised by time that arise specifically in connection with order. The key discussion occurs in IV 4, which is 28th in the chronological order, surprisingly earlier than III 7 [45]. Let me sketch the argument.

Time shows itself especially plainly in the turning of the heaven of the stars, so it might seem to derive above all from the activity of the Soul of the All. But this highlights a difficulty. Time is "divided up" (*merizomenon*), but the activity of the Soul of the All is utterly self-same and hence eternal. Can this Soul generate time, but not be *in* time? And if it is not in time, what makes it generate time, and not eternity?

In working out his earliest answer to this conundrum, Plotinus first stipulates that in fact *all* soul is eternal—not just the Soul of the All but individual souls in general, whose affections and productions are in the other-and-other of sensible motion below the heaven.[11] This yields the following series:

> The souls are eternal, and time is posterior to them, and that which is in time is less than time (for time must encompass what is in time, as, [Aristotle] says, is the case with what is in place and number).[12]

Now if the affections of the souls are in time, and hence below time proper, while the souls themselves are eternal and thus above it, time has come to be represented as "within" soul in the brute schematic sense that something of soul is on either side of it, that it reaches from soul's eternal and intellectual life to soul's time-ordered and sensible productions.

10. IV 4, 15: 3–4.

11. It is an elementary mistake in Plotinus to confuse the Soul of the All (*hê psuchê tou pantos*) with "all soul" (*pasa psuchê*), soul in general as an hypostasis. The Soul of the All is, like us, an individual soul, whose privilege is simply to have a body in which she can act without declination from eternity. She is therefore able to dispense with memory and expectation and act entirely in the present.

12. IV 4, 15: 17–20. Reference is to *Physics* IV 12, 221a12 and 28–30.

Time seems to mediate the translation of order, arrangement, from intelligible simplicity to sensible seriality. How is this to be understood?

Things in time are the showing and making of soul. In what way is the "one thing after another" of their *order* in soul? If order is real in the soul with its separateness (*to choris*), how does that not destroy the simultaneity (*to hama*) which must be equally real for soul to be eternal? And yet if order is in the soul in simultaneity and togetherness as against sensible succession, then there are *two* orders:

> . . . if the ordering principle (*to tatton*) is other than the order (*hê taxis*), it will be of such a kind *as to speak*, in a way.[13]

But just this is unacceptable. The time-order of natural process is an immediate manifestation of power, not the result of any "giving of orders" (*epistatein*) as between one thing with the power to enunciate and another with a separate power to obey. We must merge the *epistatein* into *taxis* itself.

> If that which gives orders (*to epistatoun*) is the primary arrangement (*hê prôtê taxis*), it no longer says, but only makes, this after that (*ouketi legei alla poiei monon tode meta tode*). For if it says, it does so with an eye on the arrangement (*eis taxin blepon*).[14]

To have an eye on, to view, one must stand back, stand clear of what is viewed. But the power to give orders in the case of time-ordering is the ordering itself, as immediate power.

"Does not speak but only makes." In the treatise Plotinus wrote immediately after *Difficulties About the Soul*, entitled *Nature, Contemplation, and the One* (III 8 [30]), silence itself becomes thematic. Because of its interior timelikeness, hypostatic Soul harbors a contemplative power, called Nature, which is productive in spontaneity and not by giving directions. To the question, "Why do you make?" her answer is "Shhhh . . . understand the power of my silence." I cite the whole passage:

13. IV 4, 16: 13–14, emphasis added.
14. IV 4, 16: 14–15.

You ought not to ask, but to understand in silence, you, too, just as I am silent and not in the habit of talking. Understand what, then? That what comes into being is what I see in my silence, an object of contemplation, which comes to be naturally, and that I, originating from this sort of contemplation, have a contemplative nature. My act of contemplation makes what it contemplates, as the geometers draw their figures while they contemplate. But I do not draw, but as I contemplate, the lines which bound bodies come to be *as if they fell out* (*hôsper ekpiptousai*) from my contemplation.[15]

Here, the direct spontaneity of silence, not "speaking," is supplemented by not "drawing," which stands in for the plastic arts in general. The spontaneity in which corporeal things come to be "by nature" is evoked by the expression "as if they fell out."

The verb here, *ekpiptô* (fall out), is used at a similarly pivotal moment in chapter 11 of *On Eternity and Time*. The title of the story there is "How Time First Fell Out," (*hopôs dê prôton exepese chromos*). It appears at first that Time is going to tell his story "in person." I just gave an example of how readily Plotinus personifies his "concepts." But in fact Time never does speak up, and it is "we" who wind up talking.

And so, moving on to the always 'next' and what is 'afterward' and not the same, but different into different, by making a kind of stretch of our journey we have constructed Time as an image of eternity.[16]

I have written elsewhere about the silence of time and what it means that Plotinus has "we" replace him.[17] Here, I want to seize formally on Plotinus's theme of *falling*. This is the *ecstatic* moment in his phenomenology, in the sense of ecstatic that belongs to temporal problematic. Heidegger gives the horizonal schema for this temporal ecstasis (that of the present), as "Being-alongside" (*Sein bei*).

To say that eternity and time configure a temporal ecstasis it might seem necessary to specify in which direction the standing-out or

15. III 8, 4: 3–11.
16. III 7, 11: 17–19.
17. ST 2, section 3.

standing-away takes place, from time toward eternity, or eternity toward time. This is the same question of philosophical method that Plotinus raised in the opening chapter of III 7. Since the horizonal schema is provided by falling, it is tempting to say that its "direction" as an ecstasis is "downward." But what if it is only by some kind of projection "upward" that eternity becomes thinkable in the first place, as something to fall from?

Temporal ecstases are not in, across, or from time, but "into" disclosure space. More properly, the unity of the ecstases is how the temporal disclosure space is composed. I am not going to carry that discussion beyond where I left it in chapter 1 until a second example of temporal ecstasis is available, that of Augustine. His access to temporal problematic is rooted in his original experience of memory as ecstatic *having been*, whose horizonal schema is the "already in" (*schon in*). In ways I will illustrate in the next section, this opens into a temporal phenomenology more radical than that of Plotinus.

Meanwhile, it remains to exhibit the *temporality* of the Plotinian position. Temporality means future, past, present, and in discussing them Plotinus takes his direction from what Timaeus goes on to say just after the passage at 37c–d with which I began this section. He first names days and nights and months and years, calling them "portions" or "parts" of time (*merê chronou*), then turns to "forms" or "aspects" (*eidê*) of time, of which of course there are three, elicited by the three continuous tenses: imperfect, present, and simple future. Two of them, "was" and "will be," are *generated* forms of time, while "is" alone can be predicated of the everlasting.

> 'Was' and 'will be' are generated forms of time (*chronou gegonota eidê*), which we, being oblivious, incorrectly carry over to the everlasting essence (*epi tên aïdion ousian*). For we say it was, it is, and it will be, whereas according to true discourse (*kata ton alêthê logon*) 'is' alone applies. The 'was' and the 'will be' suit the coming-to-be proceeding in time—for they are motions, but what abides forever the same is motionless. (37e, my translation)

Plotinus's most direct response to this passage is chapter 3 of III 7. He begins with questions about the everlasting and eternity:

What, then, would this be by reason of which we call the whole universe There eternal and everlasting, and what is everlastingness? Is it the same thing as, and identical with eternity, or is eternity in conformity with it? (III 7, 3:1–4)

He comes to the position that everlastingness is the substrate (*hypokeimenon*) of eternity, while eternity "shines out" (*eklampon*) as the temporal present, as what Plato had in mind in saying that "is" alone applies.

> . . . one sees eternity in seeing a life that abides in the same, and always has the all present to it, not now this, and then again that, but all things at once, and not now some things, and then again others, but a partless completion, as if they were all together in a point, and had not yet begun to go out and flow into lines; it is something which abides in the same in itself and does not change at all but is always in the present (*en tô paronti aei*), because nothing of it has passed away, nor again is there anything to come into being, but that which it is, it is; so that eternity is not the substrate but something which, as it were, shines out from the substrate itself in respect of what is called its sameness. . . . (III 7, 3:15–26)

The Platonic selection of the present for the temporality of eternity, making it the lead horizon of ecstatic temporality itself, becomes as explicit here as one could ask. On the level of "doctrine," the position conforms completely to *Timaeus* 37e, and goes beyond it mainly by way of elaboration. For example, in Plotinus, and even more readily in Iamblichus interpreting him, one can make out what Plato might mean by saying that "was" and "will be" are *motions*. That discussion brings out the characteristic temporality of time.[18]

This is all sufficiently familiar that we can move past it without additional exposition. But there is an original note sounded by Plotinus in regard to the temporality of eternity that deserves attention here. In III 7, 4 he comes again to the exclusion of "was" and "will be" from

---

18. The temporality of time in Neoplatonism is best presented in Iamblichus, whose expansion of Plotinus cannot be accommodated here. See ST 2, 2, "The Schema of Participation," 62–64.

eternity, but with supporting arguments that give a curious priority to the "will be," the future.

> Now this true whole, if it really is a whole, must not only be whole in the sense that it is all things, but it must have its wholeness in such a way that it is deficient in nothing. If this is so, there is nothing that is going to be for it, for if something is going to be, it was lacking to it before; so it was not whole. But what could happen to it contrary to its nature? For it is not affected in any way. If, then, nothing could happen to it, there is no postponement of being, and it is not going to be, nor did it come to be. Now with things which have come to be, if you take away the "will be" what happens is that they immediately cease to exist, as they are continually acquiring being; but with things which are not of this kind, if you add to them the "will be," what happens is that they fall from the seat of being. (III 7, 4:13–21)

Plotinus can be credited with insight into the priority of the future in the temporality of being in time. But equally striking is how he dramatizes the importance of excluding the future from eternity as a "true whole" (*pan alêthinon*). If you *take away the future* from things that come to be, they "immediately cease to exist" (*aei euthus hyparchei mê einai*), whereas if you *add the future* to what does not come to be, it precipitates a "fall from the seat of being" (*to errein ek tês tou einai hedras*). The verb *errô* means "be clean gone, perish, disappear" (LSJ A.II.3, referencing this passage), hence be lost, gone, fallen.

Given these strictures about ascribing anything futural to eternal true being or divine life, the clear priority of the future that Augustine finds in the human *imago dei* poses sensitive problems for any argument to the divine trinity. To uncover ecstatic having been as an independent discovery by Augustine in temporal problematic is a more straightforward task. In his trinity-image triad of memory, understanding, and will, memory (*memoria*) is the figure of the Father, understanding (*intelligentia*) that of the Son, "begotten" by the Father. Such an origin for the ecstatic present is literally beyond the Plotinian horizon.

THE EMERGENCE OF ECSTATIC MEMORY
IN *MUSIC* AND *CONFESSIONS*

In Plotinus, the topic of eternity and time leads to *soul*, either soul in general, or the world-soul in particular. For him, ecstatic presence of mind is only weakly individuated, memories and expectations having been excluded from pure contemplation. In Augustine, the topic of eternity and time leads to *individuated soul*. I find that I can keep the Plotinian identification of time for Augustine—the life of soul in a motion of transition from one way of life to another—except that for Augustine, the soul in question is individual soul, one's own soul. The temporal horizons have been drawn down into an actual lifetime. The basis for this development is *ecstatic memory*.

Augustine addresses ecstatic-horizonal having been through an original phenomenology of *memory*. What I am calling "ecstatic memory" is the aspect of his phenomenology that belongs to temporal problematic proper. This excludes memory as storage for retrieval, memorizing. Storage memory augments presence of mind, but it is essentially subordinate to it. Ecstatic memory, by contrast, is foundational for presence of mind, which is "begotten" from it in the image of the Son from the Father.

The theme only becomes explicit in those terms in *Trinity*, but the underlying problematic begins to surface already in the early dialogue *On Music*, and it is consolidated in Book X of the *Confessions*. Summarizing that evidence is the task of this section. But because of the greater directness and clarity Augustine achieved later, the first text I present is from *Trinity*.

> It appears, therefore, that the beholding of the mind (*conspectus*) is something pertaining to its nature, and that it is recalled in this nature (*in eam revocatur*) not as through places in space but by incorporeal conversion, when it thinks itself (*se cogitat*); when it does not think itself, it appears that it is not in its own sight, nor is its own perception formed from it—and yet it knows itself as though it were to inself remembrance of itself (*tamquam ipsa sibi sit memoria sui*).[19]

19. *De trinitate libri quindecim* XIV, 6, 8. Corpus Christianorum Series Latina, volume L (Books I–XII) and LA (Books XIII–XV), L, 431–32. *On the Trinity*, trans. A. West Hadden, edited and annotated by W.G.T. Shedd (Nicene and Post-Nicene Fathers, vol. III, 1–228), 187. References to *de trinitate* will henceforth cite book, chapter, and numbered paragraph (e.g., "XIV, 6, 8"), then Latin page number in the format "CCSL L, 431–32." References to the NPNF edition of the English for *On the Trinity* will have the format "OT 187." I will later be citing more frequently from the more recent translation by Edmund Hill, *The Trinity*

It is methodologically important that the striking formulation about memory with which the passage ends addresses the situation when the mind is *not* "thinking itself." Augustine was fascinated throughout his career by the problem of how one can seek to know what one doesn't know. Earlier in *Trinity*, speaking of the mind, he wrote, "For it knows itself as seeking and as not knowing itself, in that it seeks to know itself."[20] In any recalling, there has to be a calling and that which is called upon. What calls is the authentic self, here "the beholding of the mind." What is called upon is the mind "when it does not think itself," the inauthentic self so caught up in everyday care that "it supposes itself to be that without which it cannot be present to itself."[21]

Even then, the self knows itself "as though it were to itself remembrance of itself." Memory of self, *memoria sui*, is an ecstatic self-knowing, founding the possibility of hearing the call.[22]

Augustine first encounters ecstatic memory in the early dialogue in six books, *On Music*. It arrives fully only in Book VI. There, after four books of self-admittedly tedious exercises in the quantitative metrics of Latin verse, Augustine turns to a curiously groping effort at identifying, and sorting hierarchically, all the ranks of numbers involved in reciting the verse, *deus creator omnium*.[23] It is composed of four iambs, each having one short and one long syllable (double the

---

(Brooklyn: New City Press, 1991), in the format "Trin. (page number)." [There are two extant divisions of the books of *de trinitate* into chapters. CCSL and OT follow one; Trin., the other. Numbered paragraphs are not affected. I will always cite the CCSL chapter number.]

20. X, 3, 5. CCSL L, 318; OT 137.

21. X, 8, 11. CCSL L, 324; Trin. 295.

22. To the objection that memory pertains to the past, whereas what is sought is mind's capacity to be present to itself (*praesto sibi*), Augustine devotes a whole chapter of reflections on language, showing that when one says *memoria sui* of one's own *mens*, "*ad res praesentes memoria pertinet*" (memory pertains to something present). XIV, 11, 14. CCSL L, 441–42; OT 191.

23. *On Music* VI, II, 2, trans. R. C. Taliaferro. In *Saint Augustine: The Immortality of the Soul, the Magnitude of the Soul, on Music, the Advantage of Believing, on Faith in Things Unseen*. Catholic University of America Press, 1977. Hereafter the format will be "VI, II, 2. Taliaferro 326."

time of the short), hence three times, making a total of twelve.[24] The master asks:

> M.: Tell me if you will . . . , where you think the four iambs and twelve times are it consists of. Is it to be said these numbers are only in the sound heard or also in the hearer's sense belonging to the ears, or also in the act of the reciter, or, because the verse is known, in our memory, too?
>
> D.: In all of them, I think.
>
> M.: Nowhere else?
>
> D.: I don't see what else there is, unless, perhaps, there is some interior and superior power these proceed from.
>
> M.: I am not asking for what is merely suspected (*quid suspiciandum sit*).[25]

The disciple seems to want "numbers" in the musical sense to be as concrete as possible. His pious invocation of an "interior and superior power" is dismissed by the master as "something merely suspected," though in fact it is exactly what he wants to defend. On the other hand, the stubborn concreteness of the disciple compels the master to attempt demonstrations that Augustine clearly values and enjoys. The prototype of such dialogic, one that pulls him both ways, comes in Book I, early in the effort to assess the definition of music put forward by the master: *scientia bene modulandi* (the knowledge/science of modulating well).[26]

Master and disciple are agreed that music involves performance. Singers and dancers are mentioned, later lyre and flute players. What "modulating well" in performance means is that the sounds (or movements) produced have a pleasing *modus*, measure, a settled quantity.

---

24. i.e., deUS creA torOM niUM. Keep in mind that what I here show as stress needs to be understood as quantity, double that of the short syllable.

25. VI, II, 2. Taliaferro 326.

26. I, II, 2. "Modulate" has a specific meaning in music today, pertaining to moving in harmonic space, which is not Augustine's subject at all. I am keeping the term for its relation to *modus*.

Augustine calls this generically *number*. In broadest application, the discipline of music seeks to make all actions numbersome, but in Book I the focus remains on hearing music performed. What are the implications in this context of calling music a *science*, not an art?

The disciple takes it that this makes music belong to the life of *animus* (mind), but he is not convinced that a specifically bodily facility is not equally characteristic of it—namely, imitation. If, as the master seems to require, music requires reason (*ratio*), must we not allow that the science of music joins reason with imitation?

> D.: What is to prevent me from calling it science when reason is joined with imitation?
>
> M.: Since now we are concerned with the cither-player and the lute-player, that is to say with musical things, I want you to tell me whether, when such people do something by imitation, that is to be attributed to the body, that is, to a kind of bodily obedience (*obtemperationi cuidam corporis*).
>
> D.: I think it ought to be attributed to both the mind and the body, though the word which you used, 'bodily obedience', was properly enough introduced by you. For it can only obey the mind.
>
> M.: I see you are very careful in not wishing to attribute imitation to the body alone. But you won't deny that science belongs to the mind alone, will you?
>
> D.: Who would deny that?[27]

Because the mind/body (*animus/corpus*) distinction is so much the framework of the ongoing discussion, I should admit that I cannot find a better way to translate *animus* here than "mind," though I would like to reserve that for *mens*.[28] The problem is that Latin says "soul" in two

---

27. I, IV, 6–7. Taliaferro 180.

28. *Mens*, and its connection to *memini* (mind, bear in mind), is not used in *Music* or *Confessions*, but is essential to *Trinity*. Throughout this section, "mind" means *animus*.

genders: *anima, animus. Anima* stays most in touch with the root sense, which ranges from "breeze," to "breath," to "soul" as bodily aliveness. *Animus* is sometimes defined as "the rational soul", "the seat of the intellect," "sensibility," and "will." But that is definition, not translation, and here again, the word itself most immediately says "soul." Both *anima* and *animus* translate Greek *psychê* (soul) in some but not all of its uses. In my judgment, English "soul" should be reserved for *anima* in Augustine, while *animus* may be economically translated "mind." It should be stressed, however, that there is no "mind/body" problem in Augustine in any post-Cartesian sense. There are instead two dimensions of human life that need to be understood precisely in their *integration.* Writing later in Book XII of *Trinity* (as detailed in the next section), Augustine formally takes the man and the woman in Genesis 2 to be a figure for this kind of integration, which comes about within the self through wholehearted will, without a mediating third. Both the integration, and the defection to which it is exposed, involve Augustine's interpretation of the Fall, which I leave aside for now.

Here in Book I of *Music,* despite his seeing something both bodily and mental in musical imitation, the disciple feels called upon to concede that science "belongs to the mind alone." The master has identified the role of the body in imitation as a form of *compliance* (*obtemperatio,* submission, obedience), which the disciple understands as shoring up the premise that science belongs to the mind alone. But as Augustine shapes the discussion, the "bodily compliance" issue leads in an unexpected direction.

> M.: Be as attentive as possible, so that what we have been stren-uously looking for may appear. For you have already granted me that science lives only in the mind.
>
> D.: And why shouldn't I?
>
> M.: Further, do you attribute the sense of hearing to the mind, to the body, or to both?
>
> D.: To both.
>
> M.: And memory?
>
> D.: To the mind, I think. For if we perceive by the senses something we commit to memory, that is no reason to think we must consider memory to be in the body.

M.: This happens to be a great question, and one not proper to this discussion.[29]

Memory makes its entrance in *Music* in connection with observation of the role of imitation in musical performance. The disciple thinks of memory in the conventional way, as sense perceptions that "we commit to memory" (*memoriae commendamus*), store for retrieval. But just because the contents of memory are bodily perceptions, he doesn't think it follows that memory itself is a bodily function. Augustine knows that this is a "great question," but he doesn't let the master take the bait.

He presses further into the bodily compliance required for imitation. Whether this compliance is accomplished with an operation of the mind in the sense of science, i.e., intellect, or simply with a familiarity built up from memory, the body is not at all passive in this relation. The question of practice (*usus*) arises. An instrumentalist requires a kind of speed and agility in the fingers that can only come with practice. Practice produces a specifically bodily facility, even and perhaps especially when performance follows from science. Otherwise, those with more science would be the better players, which is not the case. But not only are most performers successful through imitation alone, but it is evident that clarity about the purpose of what is to be done (with the fingers, voice, etc.) does not suffice for doing it.

M.: Consider this too. For I suppose that you have sometimes noticed how artisans and craftsmen of this sort keep striking the same place with an axe or a hammer and how the blow is only carried where the mind (*animus*) intends it, and how, when we try and can't do likewise, they often ridicule us.[30]

Without long and continuing practice, the bodily facility required for expressive performance will not be available. One can know perfectly well what is to be done, and more than that, have often seen it being done. Yet no degree of intellectual perspicuity about the task and tools,

29. I, IV, 8. Taliaferro 181.
30. I, IV, 9. Taliaferro 182.

will by itself permit you to do what, say, the blacksmith does with a hammer and anvil, making horseshoes.

It is specifically mind that prevails in these actions, but a mind that is dependent on speed, strength, and agility for which the body has been trained. Is it appropriate to call music a science, when imitation and practice loom so large, not only in the nature of performance, but in its success with audiences? Augustine occupies his master and disciple with much critical fuss over what amounts to music as entertainment, which I will summarize succinctly in a moment. But I would draw attention right now to the philosophical anthropology that is emerging, and to the unexpected depth with which Augustine considers the compliance of body with mind. The practiced artisan directs the blow "not elsewhere than where the mind intends it" (*non alio quam eo quo intendit animus*). In the full weight that will come to attach to the verb *intendo* and the phrase *intentio voluntatis* (intention of the will), this is an intentionality that is only possible "in the body."

I introduced the audience for musical performance, because some of Augustine's most pointed observations about music as science are based on an assumption shared by master and disciple about popularity: that it cannot be the measure of the presence or absence of science in performers.

> M.: If all pipers, flute-players, and others of this kind have science, then I think there is no more degraded and abject discipline than this one.[31]

Performers are not being called degraded and abject themselves. The abilities they display justly meet with success, but they are not for that reason evidence of science, in either the performer or the audience. When confronted with admirable playing of pipes or cithern, we are . . .

> M.: . . . not to think that what fingers and joints do in such cases, because it is difficult for us, is done by science and meditation rather than by practice and diligent imitation.[32]

31. I, IV, 7. Taliaferro 180–81.
32. I, IV, 9. Taliaferro 183.

Practice and diligent imitation, Augustine suggests, can seem to mimic science and meditation. This much is said by way of admiration. Augustine becomes dismissive of popular performers, however, when he refers to them as "actors" (*histriones*, stage-players). The assumption he has the master voice is that these give themselves to music for the sake of fame and fortune, which is completely incompatible with science.

> M.: Therefore, when you have persuaded me or proved to me that any actor, if he has any talent, neither has developed it nor does he exhibit it to please the people for gain or fame, then I shall concede it is possible both to possess the science of music and to be an actor.[33]

The disciple shares the master's pessimism over the chances that any musician might seek science for itself, and mutters that matters are much the same in the "school of higher learning" (*de gymnasio*, Taliaferro). But he refuses to let go of the possibility the master has just allowed.

> D.: Yet if one exists, or should exist, liberal artists (*musici*, Taliaferro) are not for that reason to be despised; so why isn't it possible that actors ought sometimes to be honored? And then explain, if you will, this great discipline which now can't seem to me so degraded as you make out.[34]

Beginning a new chapter, Augustine avails himself of a Socratic dodge in the *Meno* mode:

> M.: I shall do so; or rather, you will do so. For all I shall do is question you. And by your answers, you will explain all of what you now seem to be after, without knowing it.

And they're off. The rest of Book I, and all of Books II through V are preparatory exercises for Book VI. The "great question" about memory—whether it belongs to the body or the mind or to both—

---

33. I, VI, 12. Taliaferro 187.
34. I, VI, 12. Taliaferro 187.

remains parked, though the whole discussion is shadowed by the Platonic conviction that intellectual insight is somehow *anamnêsis*, un-forgetting.

These intervening exercises are not completely arid, phenomenologically. Augustine is aware of what I call "framing," the time-framing of motion. There are motions too slow to perceive as motion, so that it is not possible to judge their numbers. Two actions that take place for a long time may be exactly in the ratio of 2 to 1, but that number cannot be apprehended directly. Those who try find they cannot "comprehend" the intervals by exercise of the judicial sense.[35]

> M.: Then the judicial numbers are also confined to certain limits of time-spans they cannot exceed in their judgments. And whatever exceeds these intervals they find no way to judge.[36]

Since it is via the judicial numbers that Augustine wants to demonstrate a role for reason in sensed numbers, their embodied confinement causes a problem: they would seem to be mortal, but reason is immortal.

Augustine has brought this problem upon himself by his probing of the "bodily compliance," built up by the diligent practice that is necessary for any kind of artful activity. The integration of intentionality with practice, of mind with body gets very well mapped in Book I of *Music*. But the corresponding "great question" about memory has been pushed aside. The disciple's answer that memory belongs to the mind, despite

---

35. The fact that the judicial numbers are horizoned in this way (Augustine says "confined") leads him to cosmological speculation:

> M. Why can't they do so? Unless it's because to each living thing in its proper kind and in its proportion with the universe is given a sense of places and times, so that even as its body is so much in proportion to the body of the universe whose part it is, and its age so much in proportion to the age of the universe whose part it is, so its sensing complies with the action it pursues in proportion to the movement of the universe whose part it is? VI, VII, 19. Taliaferro 343–44.

36. VI, VII, 18. Taliaferro 342. Note that "judging" in the sense Augustine is using it is a sensing, an apprehension of musical number, not a calculation or measurement.

the derivation of its content from what we perceive with the senses, has been left hanging.

On what basis would one want to assign memory to mind? If storage for retrieval is the identifying function of memory, that would seem to make it subordinate to perception. And the storage model remains the presumption early in Book VI.

> M.: For what else do we do when we recall to memory (*revocamus nos in memoriam*) except examine somehow what we've stored up (*quod reposuimus*)?[37]

But the question is, how is remembering itself somehow 'mental'? In what way is memory a phenomenon of mind?

Augustine realizes that the relationship between memory and mind is the reverse. Memory is not a phenomenon of mind, mind is a phenomenon of memory. Ecstatic-horizonal temporality allows him to address memory as such, and not just as the sum of what appears in it. In a tantalizing passage he compares the role of time in memory to that of space in vision, representing vision as a diffusion of rays of attention that "spring forth into the open (*in aperta emicant*)" . . .

> M.: . . . in such a way that, although the things we see are placed at a distance, they are yet quickened by the soul, . . . we are helped by their diffusion in comprehending place-spans (*ad capienda spatia locorum*); so the memory too, because it is somehow the light of time-spans (*quasi lumen est temporalium spatiorum*), so far comprehends these time-spans as in its own way it too can be projected (*in suo genere quodammodo extrudi potest*).[38]

Things we see placed at a distance "are yet quickened by our soul (*a nostra anima vegetentur*)." The "open" (*apertum*, from *aperio*, uncover, lay bare, open to view) is an *ecstatic* presence. Place itself is being grasped in its *phenomenality* ("quickened by the soul"). Corresponding to the "open"

---

37. VI, VIII, 22. Taliaferro 347.
38. VI, VIII, 21. Taliaferro 346.

for spans of place is "the light" that memory provides for spans of time. What it means for memory to be "projected" (*extrudi*, pres. inf. pass, of *extrudo*, thrust out, push forth) is that spans of time also can be grasped in their phenomenality. They are not, ahead of memory, pre-constituted yet "in the dark." Memory is both the constituting and the illuminating of "at once." This is *ecstatic* memory, foundation of the past as having-been-ness itself, ahead of any "information" about anything past it may make available.

The ecstatic character of memory emerges also in Augustine's shift of attention from the sensible contents preserved in memory to the motions themselves of the soul.

> M.: And the same soul receiving all its own motions multiplies, you might say, in itself, and makes them subject to recall. And this force it has is called memory, a great help in the everyday business of this life.[39]

Initially, the self-relation of soul to its own motions in memory is explored in the context of this everydayness, of embodiment.

> M.: But the memory not only takes in the carnal motions of the mind, and we have already spoken of these numbers, but also the spiritual numbers I shall now speak of briefly.[40]

He goes on to reveal the most far-reaching implication of understanding by defining music as *scientia*: number can be tracked "within" (*intus*) to its source in the eternal self-sameness of divine life. The ecstatic character of memory in this movement now becomes unmistakable.

> M.: Consider someone, who under another's questioning moves himself within to God (*sese intum ad deum movet*) in order to know the unchangeable truth. Unless memory hold selfsame his own movement (*nisi eumdem motum suum memoria*

39. VI, XI, 31. Taliaferro 356.
40. VI, XII, 34. Taliaferro 358.

teneat), he cannot be recalled to intuiting that truth (*ad intuendum illud verum . . . revocari*) by any outside admonition.[41]

The situation in this passage has features in common with the passage from *Trinity* with which this section began. An inauthentic self is "recalled" into its truth by a movement "within" (an incorporeal conversion) that would not be possible were not authenticity *given* in ecstatic memory. Even while not thinking itself, "it knows itself as though it were to itself remembrance of itself." Here, "outside admonitions" would be fruitless "unless memory hold selfsame his own movement." The movement in question is "within to God." Memory is able to hold this movement "selfsame" (*idem*, acc. *eumdem*) even when it has lapsed into untruth. The recalling and the moving within are *in the truth*, by way of ecstatic having been.

In the first half of Book X of *Confessions*,[42] Augustine revisits the levels of memory laid out in *Music*. Apart from a reflection on forgetting,[43] no new themes emerge. The identification of memory with mind (*animus*, throughout), however, becomes newly explicit.

> The mind is the very memory itself. . . . We call memory itself the mind.[44]

> Where is my recognition located but in memory itself? Surely memory is present to itself through itself, and not through its own image.[45]

Toward the close of the treatment, Augustine uses the term *memoria* in a way that translator Henry Chadwick correctly sees amounts to "consciousness":

> But where in my consciousness (*in memoria mea*), Lord, do you dwell? . . . Why do I ask in which area of my memory you dwell, as if there

41. VI, XII, 36. Taliaferro 361, extensively adapted.
42. Augustine, *Confessions*, trans. Henry Chadwick, X, i, 1–xxvii, 38.
43. X, xvi, 24–25.
44. *animus sit etiam ipsa memoria . . . . ipsam memoriam vocantes animum.* X, xiv, 21. Chadwick 191.
45. X, xv, 23. Chadwick 192.

really are places there? Surely my memory is where you dwell, because I remember you since first I learnt of you, and I find you there when I think about you.[46]

Observations like these represent a consolidation of the insights gained in *Music*, but they do not themselves constitute a breakthrough. Ecstatic memory is not a theme in *Confessions* but a method, indeed that of the whole project.

In the narrated Books I–IX, Augustine is seeking to know what I would call his "eternal aspect," his standing in the eyes of God. His focus is on the will, the *voluntas*. This is not the same as conscious intention expressed in a choice. For, whatever passage of his life he might recall from memory, he would recall both what he thought his intentions were at the time and what he now sees was his true will.

Augustine says in one place, "Blessedness is that a man might live as he will." But for him, the problem of the will is not whether he has access to unconstrained choices (*liberum arbitrium*, free choice), but *what does he will*? Does he find in himself anything to which he can give himself wholeheartedly, anything perfectly voluntary? No; he finds a divided will, *con-cupiscentia*. Wholeheartedness is the gift of God, and Augustine looks for it in what he learns he has been truly doing, as he works within the memory loop he has constructed.

In recollections of his early life, the distance is large between what he thought he was doing then and what he now sees God was (and is still) doing in him. As he comes toward Monica's death and his ordination, that distance closes, so that finally, in the very writing of *Confessions*, the ecstatic having been of the exercise of memory gives rise to the ecstatic presence of God in prayer and confession—these two together in the ecstatic future of love, the *donum dei*, Holy Spirit as the gift of God.

I call this a phenomenology of revelation. For Augustine in *Confessions* it was immediate experience. It gets worked out explicitly as a temporal problematic in *Trinity*, as becomes apparent when it is viewed in juxtaposition with the temporal problematic of *Being and Time*.

46. X, xxv, 36. Chadwick 200–201.

TEMPORAL INTERPRETATION AND THE *IMAGO DEI*
IN *TRINITY*: METHODOLOGICAL PREPARATION

In *Being and Time*, Heidegger does not attempt an explicitly temporal
interpretation of the care-structure developed in the first division until
after he has completed intricate argumentation about method at the
opening of the second division. One issue pertains to whether Dasein
can ever be accessible as a whole, and this is resolved by the amply
familiar discussion of the anticipation of death (*Vorlaufen in den Tod*).
More complex and more readily misunderstood is the theme of
conscience, in which Dasein is portrayed as issuing a call to itself.
Hearing the call of conscience must not only be possible for Dasein in
some general, conceptual way, it must be attested, accessible existentiell
for Dasein in everydayness. The phenomenology of Dasein must be
rooted in everydayness, yet the phenomenon being sought is Dasein in its
authenticity.[47]

A closely analogous problem arises for Augustine. Corresponding to
the theme of authenticity in Heidegger is Augustine's identification of
human being, in so far as it answers to the creator's intention, as *imago
dei*. This amounts to saying, human being in its truth. Since God the
creator is trinity, it is schematically preestablished that the image of God
will feature a trinity-pattern, but before proposing any such triad—and
indeed as a necessary first step toward developing one—Augustine must
confront the fact that "first of all and mostly" human being is not found
in the truth. It is found instead eclipsed by entity not like itself, namely
corporeal things. "Held fast with anxious care (*impensa cura teneantur*),"
the human soul has become "entangled (*implicata*) with them by a kind
of daily familiarity (*diuturna quadem familiaritate*)."[48] *Diuturnus*, stem
dies (day), means "daily." Dictionaries give "of long duration, lasting,
long" (Lewis and Short), but this must be understood in the sense of
tedium, as opposite to *aeternus,* which evokes immediacy and intensity.
"A certain daily familiarity" brings out the empty flatness of the
everyday, and is certainly how one could translate Heidegger's
"everydayness" (*Alltäglichkeit*) into Latin.

47. The implications of this problem for method were discussed in detail in
chapter 1.

48. *Trin.* X, V, 7, lines 18 and 27–28. See notes 53 and 54 below for full passage.

In what follows I outline the methodological challenges of beginning from everydayness, as they arise for Augustine, in two steps.

Step One: The Essence of Truth

For Augustine, I have said, human being is not directly given "in the truth." An early task of Book VIII, which begins the "more interior way" of the second half of the treatise, is therefore stipulation as to the essence of truth. The core claim is the following:

> In regard to the essence of truth, to be true is the same as to be (*hoc est verum esse quod est esse*).[49]

The foundation for this claim is that Augustine thinks of "true" as luminous, disclosed. Augustine himself forces an interpretation of truth as disclosure—despite the fact that he, writing Latin, is actually saying *verus* and *vere* and *veritas* (from an Indo-European stem with the sense of "faithful," "pledged," "trustworthy"). The extent to which this non-Greek student of Platonism overtly calls attention to the unveiling character of the essence of truth, in order to ensure that his ontology be understood correctly, is for me striking vindication of Heidegger's treatment of *alêtheia*—and indeed the doorway into the phenomenological dimension of Augustine's whole philosophy.

A characteristic passage a chapter later is impressively explicit on this point.

> Behold and see [*ecce vide*], if thou canst, O soul (*anima*) pressed down by the corruptible body, and weighed down by earthly thoughts, many and various; behold and see, if thou canst, that God is truth. For it is written that "God is light"; not in such a way as these eyes see, but in such a way as the heart sees, when it is said, he is truth. Ask not what is truth, for immediately the darkness of corporeal images and the clouds of phantasms will put themselves in the way, and disturb that calm which at the first twinkling shone forth [*diluxit*] to you when I said truth. See that thou remainest, if thou canst, in that first twinkling with which thou art dazzled, as it were, by a flash [*coruscatione*

---

49. VIII, 1, 2. CCSL L, 270; OT 116.

perstringeris], when it is said to thee, truth. But thou canst not; thou wilt glide back to those usual and earthly things.[50]

Why not simply regard this outburst as a lapse from conceptual rigor, a decoration rather than a methodological commitment? It is obviously not argument. In context, Augustine seems to capitulate to frustration. He has been trying for three paragraphs to explain why, in order to understand God who is the truth of everything true, one must withdraw from things corporeal and changeable in their truth, and even from the spiritual creature, however glorious (e.g., the angels animating the celestial lights). Then, suddenly, he abandons analysis for the challenge recorded above. In it he assumes that we know the essence of truth to be an unveiling or a "flash"—otherwise he could not expect us to experience anything when he thunders, "Truth!" On what grounds could one judge that in this question-begging interlude of poetry there is a feature of Augustine's fundamental ontology, a feature that proves parallel to Heidegger?

First of all, after confronting us with the mystery, "God is *truth*," he straightaway alludes to the scripture, "God is *light*, in whom there is no darkness" (1 John 1:5). This would be a puzzling association were it not that the essence of truth made itself immediately available to him in terms of metaphors of light, and in particular of the unveiling of the luminous. The interpretation of that passage by Christian Platonists as pertaining to the essence of truth, and of God who is the truth, seems to be a highly coherent tradition. Consider the following passage with which Origen begins his treatment of the divine essence in *Peri Archôn*:

> I would ask [those who would maintain that God is a body] what they have to say about this passage of scripture, "God is light," as John says in his epistle, "God is light, and in him there is no darkness." He is that light, surely, which lightens the whole understanding of those who are capable of receiving truth, as it is written in the thirty-fifth psalm, "In thy light shall we see light." For what other light of God can we speak of, in which a man sees light, except God's spiritual power, which when it lightens a man causes him either to see clearly

50. VIII, 2, 3. CCSL L, 271; OT 117 (Trin. 243).

the truth of all things, or to know God himself who is called the truth?[51]

Augustine is completely in accord with this way of construing the meaning of the divine truth and of its relation to the "sight of the mind," as the following citation (easily multiplied a hundredfold) establishes:

We behold, then, by the sight of the mind [*visu mentis*], in that eternal truth from which all things temporal are made, the form according to which we are, and according to which we do anything by true and right reason, either in ourselves, or in things eternal.[52]

For us to *see* in the truth, truth must be from its very essence what I call "disclosure space," a region of illumination. The fact that the metaphoric vocabulary surrounding Augustine's discussion of truth speaks so constantly and overtly of light and sight, of appearing and obscuring, together with the explicit and emphatic association of these metaphors with the essence of the divine presence, makes it impossible not to recognize the Greek sense pointed out by Heidegger.

Yet Augustine has intimated in the last passage something even more far-reaching methodologically than the interpretation of divine truth as disclosedness, which he shares with Origen. In the eternal unhiddenness that is the divine essence, we behold the "form" according to which we *are*, i.e., our essence. We understand what it means for us "to be" only when we become available to ourselves for a "sight," which sees in the same disclosedness as defines the divine essence. This of course coheres with the guiding thesis of the treatise: that man is an image of God so "close" to the divine essence as to incorporate an image of its trinity. But more important, Augustine's handling of the essence of truth allows him to interpret this closeness with optical metaphors—specifically, with images in mirrors. From the very beginning of Book VIII, where he invokes the essence of truth as unveiling, he has his eyes on 1 Cor. 13:12, "Now we see in a mirror in an enigma, but then face to face," and 2 Cor. 3:18:

51. *Peri Archôn* I, 1, 1.
52. IX, 7, 12. CCSL L, 303–4; OT 130.

[B]ut we all, with unveiled face, beholding as in a mirror the glory of the Lord, are being changed into that same image, from glory to glory, as by the Spirit of the Lord.[53]

If the purchase on the ontology of human being-toward-God (Heidegger's phrase) that becomes available to Augustine as a result of his treatment of the essence of truth as disclosure is neglected, the argument of *Trinity* cannot even be followed, much less accurately interpreted, and the strategy of its appeal to scripture will never challenge or inform modern conceptions of theological method. Because truth is disclosure; because God is a truth that confers its power of illumination upon us as though we were an image in a mirror held before him— because of this alone does it become possible for Augustine to pursue theology as phenomenology—as a description of consciousness as it appears for itself in its own self-constituting disclosedness.

Step Two: Authenticity and Everydayness

At the start of the preceding section, I sketched Augustine's version of Heidegger's proviso that because human being is care, it is not encountered directly in its truth, but rather in a condition called everydayness. Augustine puts this situation into a mythic context, in a passage about an ontologically consequential "falling" (whose debt to Plotinus I will seek to make evident by presenting parallel passages). It comes from Book X, in which Augustine arrives at the final schema for trinitarian phenomenology: *memoria, intelligentia, voluntas*. The Plotinian prototype opens the positive exposition of time in *On Eternity and Time*. I place it in the left hand column below,[54] with Augustine's adaptation[55] on the right, as shown in the accompanying two-column list.

53. My trans., both passages.

54. III, 7, 11: 14–17, 19–33 (trans. Armstrong/Manchester). This is not the place to take up the question whether, or to what extent, Plotinus has a "myth of the fall." I address this at length in "Time and the Soul in Plotinus," chapter 2 of *The Syntax of Time*.

55. X, 5, 7. CCSL L, 320–21; OT 138, with omissions (trans. A. West Hadden). The subject of the narration throughout is *mens*. From where I stopped, the passage continues, "For we see that we have those parts of the soul (*illas partes*

Plotinus, *On Eternity and Time,* 11	Augustine, *On Trinity,* Bk. X
14 There was a busy (doing many things, *polypragmenê*) Nature,	. . . for it does many things . . . , as though in forgetfulness of itself.
wanting to control herself and be on her own, and choosing to seek for more than the present. She moved, and so did he [Time].	And because these things are corporeal, which it loved externally through the carnal senses; and because it has become entangled [*implicata*] with them by a kind of daily familiarity [*diuterna quadem familiaritate*], and yet cannot carry those corporeal things themselves with itself internally as it were into the region of incorporeal nature; therefore it combines certain images of them, and thrusts them thus made from itself into itself. For it gives to the forming of them somewhat of its own substance, yet preserves the while something by which it may judge freely of the species of those images; and this something is more properly the mind (*mens*), that is, the rational understanding, which is preserved that it may judge.
20 For because there was a certain Power of the Soul, not at rest, who wanted to be always transferring what she saw there to something else, she did not want the whole to be present to her all together; and, as from a resting seed the Logos, unfolding himself, advances, as he thinks, to muchness, but does away with the muchness by division and, instead of keeping his unity in himself, squanders it outside himself and so goes forward to a weaker extension;	
. . . [lines 17–19 omitted]	
in the same way she, making the world of sense in imitation of that other world, moving with a motion which is not that which exists there, but like it, and intending to be an image of it, first of all "be-timed" herself [*heautên echronôsen,* a neologism], instead of eternity making there to be Time, and thereupon handed over to what comes to be a being in service to Time, by making the whole of it be in Time and encompassing all its ways with Time.	

---

animae) which are informed by the likenesses of corporeal things, in common also with beasts." In the context of that contrast, *mens* and *sensus* are both "parts" of the *anima*.

I have already defended the propriety of characterizing the state of self-entanglement evoked here by Augustine with Heidegger's term "everydayness." At the outset of the passage, he also calls it a "forgetfulness of self." I note again that forgetfulness of self is not absence of self. In this Augustine finds a second major methodological opportunity: he believes he can establish the active presence of an "unknown mind."

Returning to Book VIII after the discussion of truth, Augustine recasts the situation in terms of God as the *good*. In an early summary, he writes:

> That is how we should love God, not this or that good, but good itself, and we should seek the good of the soul (*animae*), not the good it can hover over in judgment, but the good it can cleave to in love, and what is this but God?[56]

He brings out the special intimacy of soul's relationship to the good in love by contrasting it with the relative detachment of the act of intellect, which "hovers over" (*supervolitet*) its object "in judgment" (*iudicando*). The good is what "it can cleave to in love" (*cui haereat amando*). For this relationship neither "object" nor "subject" are appropriate terms. The situation is not epistemological but ontological.

> So the good the soul (*animus*) turns to in order to be good is the good from which it gets its being soul at all (*a quo habet ut animus sit*).[57]

By consequence, while there can be a turning of will away from God toward corporeal entanglements and the everyday, this cannot efface the being turned toward God that is presupposed by existence itself. What

---

56. VIII, 2, 4. CCSL L, 272; Trin. 244.

57. VIII, 2, 5. CCSL L, 274; Trin. 245. Even though the text to which the previous note attaches reads *animae* for "of the soul," without demurrer from the apparatus, the topic here and throughout this chapter is *animus*, which would call for *animi*. I discuss the challenge posed by Latin having a pair of terms for "soul," differing morphologically only in gender, above. Given the evidence that Augustine in this context is not stressing the lexical difference between the two (which in other contexts can be significant), I do not challenge Edmund Hill's translation of *animus* as "soul."

are the implications of this situation for understanding religious conversion, coming to faith?

In a new chapter, Augustine formulates the familiar vicious circle. The foundation for religious conversion is the first commandment: love God. We cannot love what we do not know. Ahead of conversion, knowledge of God would seem to be the very thing lacking. But with respect to knowledge of God, the apostle Paul makes an essential distinction:

> For since we are still *walking by faith and not by sight* (2 Cor. 5:7) we do not yet see God, as the same apostle says, *face to face* (1 Cor. 13:12). Yet unless we love him even now, we shall never see him. But who can love what he does not know? Something can be known and not loved, but I am asking whether something can be loved which is unknown, because if it cannot, then no one loves God before he knows him. And what does knowing God mean but beholding him and firmly grasping him with the mind (*mente*)?[58]

The apostle stipulates that we do not now have knowledge of God in the sense of sight or beholding, but that in place of that, there is *faith*.

A certain homiletic enthusiasm can set in at this point, extolling the witness of scripture and the faith it awakens, and Augustine certainly does not let the opportunity pass. But what seizes my interest is that through the rest of the chapter, he returns *three times* to the proviso that faith *must not*—so obviously *can*—be fictive, feigned (*ficta*, 1 Tim. 1:5).

> But naturally the spirit (*animus*) which believes what it does not see must be on guard (*cavendum est*) against fabricating something that does not exist (*fingat sibi aliquid quod non est*), and hence hoping in and loving something false.[59]

He raises the issue a second time when he allows that a certain degree of fabrication is inevitable with regard to historical matters, such as what Paul or Christ or the Virgin Mary looked like, or how miracles or the resurrection are to be imagined.

58. VIII, 4, 6. CCSL L, 274–75; Trin. 246.
59. *Loc. cit.*

When we believe some material or physical facts we read or hear about but have not seen, we cannot help our imaginations fabricating (*fingat sibi animus*) something with the shape and outline of bodies as it may occur to our thoughts, and this will either not be true, or if it is true, which can only happen extremely rarely, this is not what it profits us to hold on faith.[60]

What is held on faith is based on the witness of scripture, and distinguishing what is "material or physical" in that witness is essential for identifying what is necessary for faith. That God became man is necessary for faith; what he looked like is not.

So too with his miraculous powers and his resurrection; we know what omnipotence is and so we believe these things of the omnipotent God, and we think about them in terms of the species and genera of things which are either connatural to us, or gathered from our experience of this sort of facts (*experientia collecta de factis huiuscemodi*), and in this way our faith is not fabricated.[61]

It would be diverting to wonder what Augustine has in mind when he speaks of the "sort of facts" that we "experience," but his vagueness about it is of a piece with his hurry to dismiss the whole line of thought. Since it is precisely here that historical criticism of the "witness of scripture," embracing Humean skepticism, finds traditional (i.e., naive) orthodox faith to be in greatest peril, Augustine's briskness may seem surprising.

But his real investment against "fabricated faith" is in another dimension altogether.

Since we desire to understand as far as it is given to us the eternity and equality and unity of the trinity, and since we must believe before we can understand, we must take care our faith is not fabricated/feigned (*ne ficta sit*). This is the trinity we are to enjoy in order to live in bliss; but if we have false beliefs about it, our hope is vain and our charity is

---

60. VIII, 4, 7. CCSL L, 275; Trin. 246.
61. VIII, 4, 7. CCSL L, 276–77; Trin. 247.

not chaste. How then are we to love by believing this trinity which we do not know?[62]

The kinds of special and generic knowledge we bring to bear in thinking of the human person of the apostle Paul are of no avail here. Do we know anything about the divine trinity because we know what "three" is?

But then this is not what we love. We can always have that when we want, simply by flashing three fingers, to say nothing else. Perhaps then what we love is not what any trinity is but the trinity that God is. So what we love in the trinity is what God is. But we have never seen or known another God, because God is one, he alone is God whom we love by believing, even though we have not yet seen him. What we are asking though, is from what likeness or comparison of things known to us we are able to believe, so that we may love the as yet unknown God.[63]

The challenge for being "able to believe" is that faith be not fabricated. Despite the transcendence and uniqueness of God, Augustine still seeks "likeness or comparison of things known to us" for guidance.

Beginning again a new chapter, he returns to what functions almost as the official instance of the relation of the witness of scripture to the awakening of faith: his love for the apostle Paul. "So come back a step or two with me, and let us consider why we love the apostle."[64] Augustine says we love him "for his just mind" (*animum justum*). This leads to an analysis so familiar since Descartes, that I need outline it in a summary way. What "mind" (*animus* throughout) is, we know directly, since we each have one. How we know the mind of another is by analogy. We know firsthand how the presence of "life and soul" (*vita et anima*) expresses itself in bodily motion, and so we register the presence of soul in another by spontaneous inference—even the beasts do the same toward one another and us. "They perceive it immediately and readily, by a kind of natural affinity, from our body movements."

62. VIII, 5, 8. CCSL L, 277–78; Trin. 247.
63. VIII, 5, 8. CCSL L, 278–79; Trin. 248.
64. VIII, 6, 9. CCSL L, 279; Trin. 248.

So we know anyone else's mind from our own, and from our own we believe any mind we do not know. Indeed we are not only aware of mind but we are even able to know what mind is from a consideration of our own; for we have a mind.[65]

But the question then becomes, how do we know what "just" is, we who are not yet just? If we only know a just man by being just ourselves, so that nobody loves the apostle but the just man, "how can someone wish to be just who is not yet? Nobody wishes to be something he does not love."

> But in order for someone who is not yet just to be so, he must of course wish to be just; and in order to wish it he must love the just man. But he cannot love the just man if he does not know what 'just' is. So even the man who is not so yet knows what 'just' is.[66]

But where has he learned this from if not from himself? If to be just is a kind of beauty of the mind, it cannot be something we have seen outside of ourselves. It must therefore be something we discover in ourselves.

> What is wonderfully surprising is that a mind should see in itself (apud se) what it has seen nowhere else, and see something true, and see something true that is a just mind, and be itself mind, and not be the just mind which it sees in itself. Is there then another just mind in the mind that is not yet just?[67]

This is the unknown mind, which knows itself as not knowing itself, in that it seeks to know itself. It is this seeking, the capacity to be moved by love, that announces the presence of "another mind."

Announcing this result at the start of this discussion, I used the phrase "active presence of an 'unknown mind'." "Wishing to be just" follows upon loving the just man: ". . . in order to wish it he must love the just man." Since we know the just man to love him from the

---

65. VIII, 6, 9. CCSL L, 279–80; Trin. 249.
66. *Loc. cit.*
67. VIII, 6, 9. CCSL L, 282; Trin. 250.

"unknown" just man in ourselves, "wishing to be just" in Augustine is equivalent to "being willing to have a conscience" (*Gewissenhabenwohlen*) in Heidegger.[68] It is the active presence, in everydayness, of authenticity as *possible*. Human authenticity (here, for Augustine, the just mind; later, the image of God) is possible—factically possible—and this is *attested existentiell*.

TEMPORAL INTERPRETATION AND THE *IMAGO DEI* IN *TRINITY*: PHENOMENOLOGICAL PARALLELS

While the discussion of mind in relation to truth, and in a particular way in relation to itself, have both been steps along the "more inward way" (*modo interiore*)[69] that Book VIII promises for the second half of the treatise, the distinctive inner or "psychological" trinities only arrive in Books IX and X. Book VIII closes by advancing a trinity-schema, but while it is of service in developing the inner trinity of Book IX, it is not itself a structure of inwardness, but something more general. I want to follow closely how it arises.

Early in the final chapter of Book VIII, the "more inward" theme of the second half is touched on again. Those who seek God through the powers that rule the world are going in the wrong direction:

[T]hey are trying to go by an outer route and forsaking their own inwardness, where God is present more inwardly still (*quibus interior est deus*).[70]

The vector that points within is love, and this remark leads into a peroration on love. Augustine argues that love of brother and love of God do not compete, because he who loves his brother loves love, and God is love.

Let no one say, "I don't know what to love." Let him love his brother, and love that love; after all, he knows the love he loves with better than

---

68. For discussion, including my rejection of Macquarrie/Robinson's "wanting-to-have-a- conscience," see chapter 1.

69. VIII, Prooem, 1. CCSL L, 269; Trin. 242.

70. VIII, 7, 11. CCSL L, 285; Trin. 252.

the brother he loves. There now, he can already have God better known to him than his brother, certainly better known because more present, better known because more inward to him, better known because more sure. Embrace love, which is God, and embrace God with love.[71]

After expanding on this inward-pointing series (brother-self-love-God), he comes at length to the final paragraph of Book VIII and the question, what is love? His answer is a threesome.

> Now love means someone loving and something loved with love. There you are with three, the lover, what is being loved, and love. And what is love but a kind of life coupling or trying to couple together two things, namely lover and what is being loved?[72]

The extreme generality of this triad should be appreciated. As Augustine himself notes, it applies to love in the flesh as well as the mind-to-mind love of friendship. Nothing has yet been found out about the trinity which God is, but perhaps love is the place to look. "It provides us as it were with the frame of a kind of warp on which we can weave what remains to be said."[73]

Book IX sets out to illustrate the threesome of love not directly with Father, Son, and Holy Spirit, but rather with that image, "disparate, but image nonetheless" (*impari imagine attamen imagine*),"[74] which is human being. Augustine tells us it will be easier to start with the image because we are it. Here we have what Heidegger calls the ontic/ontological priority of finite existence for the phenomenology of Dasein. Like

---

71. VIII, 8, 12. CCSL L, 286; Trin. 253. Trin. writes, "Let him love his brother, and love that love," reading imperative *diligat*. In n. 39 *ad loc.* (257), E. Hill explains why he amends the best text reading, *diliget*, "and he will love." "The argument here requires that this love too be made an imperative, and not a consequence of the preceding imperative." I disagree. But the entailment here is not a matter of sequence, so I am citing the Trin. passage as printed.

72. VIII, 10, 14. CCSL l, 290–91; Trin. 255.

73. *Loc. cit.*

74. IX, 2, 2. CCSL L, 294; Trin. 271.

Heidegger, Augustine exploits this priority in what amounts to a concrete procedure, the phenomenology itself.

He considers the distinctions in love as pertaining to mind (*mens*) in relation to itself. Take mind, and mind's love of itself. These two are each mind itself, that is, mind as a whole, and yet they differ as relative to one another. In this they answer to the predicate logic Augustine develops in Books V–VII. Anything said of God in relation to himself is predication by substance or essence, and is unitary. Anything predicated by relation, as Father begets, Son is begotten, is said neither by substance nor *accidens*, accidentally. Predication by relation predicates severally, giving a plurality, yet not as something merely incidental to unitary substance.

So Augustine begins with mind and mind's self-love. These so far are only two; where is a third? Love is for what is known. If the mind knows itself, there are then another two, mind and its knowledge of itself. So now there are three: mind, mind's knowledge of itself, mind's love of itself. These are said severally in relation to one another, but each is mind as a whole, and substance. This is the first sketch of a trinitarian image of God, accessible phenomenologically.

I have stated the argument with extreme compression in order to get to an objection to the terms of the position itself. It amounts to a refusal to follow the most explicit and deliberate language Augustine uses. Construing the argument phenomenologically is blocked again and again.

To set the supposedly objectionable sentences in their full context, I return to his first step in unfolding the trinity of love in the mind, when it was just the dyad mind and love, and highlight some text.

> When the mind loves itself, it reveals two things, mind and love. . . .
> And if love is a substance, it is certainly not body but spirit (*spiritus*),
> just as mind too is not body but spirit. Love and mind however are not
> two spirits but one spirit, not two beings but one being; and yet they
> are two somethings, lover and love, or if you like beloved and loved.
> And these are called two things relatively to one another. . . . Mind and
> spirit however are not said relatively but state being.[75]

75. IX, 2, 2. CCSL L, 295; Trin. 272.

To the clause "if love is a substance" Edmund Hill attaches a footnote that begins:

> Augustine's use of Aristotle's ten categories in Book V makes it clear that he does not really think of love as a substance, and knows perfectly well that in our normal use of the word we mean by it an act, a quality, or a relationship.[76]

"He does not really think of love as a substance." This has been going on in editions of *de trinitate* in English since at least 1887, when W.G.T. Shedd revised and annotated Arthur West Hadden's translation for the Nicene and Post-Nicene Fathers of the Church. To this entire chapter, he attaches the following footnote:

> Augustin here begins his discussion of some ternaries that are found in the Finite, that illustrate the trinality of the Infinite. Like all finite analogies, they fail at certain points. In the case chosen—namely the lover, the loved, and love—the first two are substances, the last is not. The mind is a substance, but its activity in loving is not. In chapter iv, 5, Augustin asserts that "love and knowledge exist substantially, as the mind itself does." But no psychology, ancient or modern, has ever maintained that the agencies of a spiritual substance or entity are themselves spiritual substances or entities. The activities of the human mind in cognizing, loving, etc., are only its energizing, not its substance.[77]

"No psychology, ancient or modern"—except this one. The phenomenology of spiritual substance that *Trinity* presents explicitly distances itself from the ontology of the corporeal thing, above all from the subject/act dichotomy. To clarify what I find to be the phenomenological moment in Books VIII, IX, and X, it will be helpful to review the literary-historical structure of the treatise as a whole.

De trinitate is a complex literary entity. In its relevance for Augustine's intellectual biography, it falls into four compositional segments:

76. Note 9 *ad loc.*, Trin. 282.
77. OT n. 2, 126.

Books I–IV, composed between 400 and 406, containing a review of the traditional orthodox schema with defense against the typical misreadings of scriptural ambiguities.

Book VIII, composed in 407, which introduces the possibility of a *modo interiore* (more inward way), than what preceded it. At this point, that would have been just the doctrinal expositions of Bks. I–IV.

Books V–VII and IX–XII, composed from 413 to 416, in which the theory of predication by relation and its illustration from trinities in the mind is first worked out.

Books XIII–XV, composed from 418 to 421, in which the strategy of "ascent" through the trinities of the mind is brought back into relation with scripture and given formal theological context and evaluation from the point of view of revelation and Augustine's constructive metaphysics of the divine eternity.[78]

I call attention to the fact that the *predicate logic* (Bks. V–VII) and the introduction to the *trinity of the mind* (in Bks. IX–X) are being composed at the same time. They either draw on the same insight, or comprise one.

Book V (VI and VII are ancillary) does not "make use of Aristotle's ten categories" (Hill). *Categories* had always been hyped to him, Augustine reports, as some kind of mountain to be scaled, but when he finally looked into the matter, he found it trivial.[79] All he makes use of is the general distinction between substance and accident, so that he can be rigorous in explaining how predication by *relation* is *not accidental with God*. There can be plural eternal relations in the divine life, without compromising the unity of predication by substance. To say the Father begets, the Son is begotten, the Spirit proceeds, is to speak of three. But anything said of God in relation to himself is singular. To say the Father is eternal, the Son is eternal, the Spirit is eternal, is just to say one thing three times: God is eternal.

This same pattern, with completely parallel motivations, is foregrounded in Book IX. In Book V, the triad in question is specific:

---

78. Following Eugene TeSelle, *Augustine the Theologian*. New York: Herder and Herder, 1970.

79. Cf. *Confessions* IV, 28.

Father, Son, Spirit. In Book IX, Augustine wants the triad of the mind to be specific as well. In the introductory sketch he gives in this book, to be improved upon in Book X, they are mind, self-knowledge, self-love. To readers who will not entertain the assertion that knowledge and love are substantial, and substantial *in the same way as mind*, it can seem that any triad "selected" from the activities of the mind is intrinsically arbitrary. Shedd's last line again:

> The activities of the human mind in cognizing, loving, etc., are only its energizing, not its substance.

The effect of the "etc." after "cognizing and loving" is to suggest there are numberless other "activities of the mind" that might just as well have been selected. The implication is that the choice of just these two is arbitrary. That said, cognizing and loving do not, in any case, make a triad with mind, since mind alone is substance. Nothing is allowed to disturb the isolation of substance, the subject of its activities.

But what if *mind itself* is an "energizing," and substance *in that very way*? In the first place, this is just canonical Aristotle. "Energizing" is a nice translation for Aristotle's neologism *energeia*. This is built from *ergon* (act, deed). A parallel built in English gives "enactment." Substance (*ousia*, essence) is the enactment of a "what-it-was-to-be" (*to ti ên einai*), of a form (*eidos*). Mind is activity, enactment, in a primal sense, known to Aristotle as the first mover, the divine life.

Mind, self-knowledge, self-love, have got to be a proper threesome for Augustine, so he cannot allow them to be sundered across a substance/activity divide. This becomes unmistakable in the transition to Book X, where the final schema for the trinity in mind as the image of God is introduced: *memoria, intelligentia, voluntas*, (memory, understanding, will). This is the same trinity reached in Book IX, just stated more radically and productively for phenomenology, in that its intrinsically *temporal* character becomes accessible.

How do the terms of Book X relate to those of Book IX? *Voluntas* corresponds to self-love, *intelligentia* to self-knowledge. Are they perhaps "faculties" for the corresponding activities—will, the faculty for loving, understanding, the faculty for knowing? If something like that is right, then memory would be the faculty for "mind"-ing, the first act of the mind. And that is exactly right. Here, the ecstatic memory, whose early traces I have sketched above, comes into its own. Here also, Latin *mens* takes over from *animus* as the term most likely to be behind a translator's "mind."

Augustine is keenly aware of the derivation of *mens*, mind, from *memini*, "remember" in the sense of "mind" in the expressions, "Bear in mind" or "Mind your mother!" It suggests the past as what Heidegger calls "having-been-ness" (*Gewesenheit*), which is not "passed" but a disclosure-character of the situation "now," into which the self has been "thrown." In *Being and Time*, this disclosure character or "existential" is called "disposition" (*Befindlichkeit*). It is the analogy to mind in Augustine's trinity-image.

In the move from Book IX to Book X, a temporal character most obviously attaches to the first member of the triad, memory. But Heidegger begins his temporal interpretation of the care-structure with a decided emphasis on the precedence of the future, the horizon for the ecstasis that is existence itself. Future in German is "advent" (*Zukunft*, a coming-toward). The disclosure character or existential for this he calls "understanding" (*Verstehen*). As "projection" (*Entwurf*) or "anticipation" (*Vorlaufen*), the "horizonal schema" for understanding is the "ahead-of-itself" (*sich vorweg*). Dasein "comes toward" itself from out of an ahead-of-itself that it already *is*. In unity with "already in" (*schon in*, the horizonal schema for having been), and "alongside" (*bei*, the horizonal schema for the present), the "ahead-of-itself already-in as being-alongside" of existence schematizes the phenomenon of ecstatic-horizonal temporality itself: future, past, present.

> The character of "having been" arises from the future, and in such a way that the future which "has been" (*gewesene*) (better, which is "having been-ing," *gewesende*) releases from itself the present (*Gegenwart*). This phenomenon, unified as a having-been-ing presentifying future (*dergestalt als gewesend-gegenwärtigende Zukunft*), we call *temporality* (*die Zeitlichkeit*).[80]

80. Division II, chapter 3, section 65. SZ 326; BT 374. My translation.

The position summarized here is the keystone for Heidegger's *temporal interpretation* of the everydayness of care in Division Two, Chapter 4. Because this formulation encapsulates an entire, fully worked out temporal problematic, I will choose it over Augustine's at best incipient one to point this chapter toward its conclusion.

Something needs to be clear about temporal interpretation itself. Temporal interpretation does not take something independently presented as well understood about past/present/future and "apply it" to the exposition of arguments in Heidegger and Augustine. Just the reverse. It seeks to learn *what to mean by* "the future," by "the past," by "the present," *from those arguments.*

Heidegger's temporal problematic emerges from the phenomenology of anticipatory resoluteness in II, 1 and 2. Its distinctive features are well represented in the formula he constructs, *gewesend-gegenwärtigende Zukunft.* The third term, the future, functions as the unity of the first two. It is the noun, the other two are participial adjectives. Dynamically, the future takes the lead in what Augustine calls the "turn within." The corresponding moment in Heidegger is attesting *existentiell* the possibility of authenticity. When I say future, past, present are a trinity, not just a triad, I have in mind these two key features of ecstatic temporality that I learn from *Being and Time.*

Turning to Augustine, I have indicated that I would not force any simply assertoric association of memory/understanding/will with past/present/future. Temporal interpretation of the argument along "the more inward way" must prove suitable from within the argument itself. Now, the trinity of the mind was never going to be a static model for Augustine. It was meant to serve dynamically in the mapping of a series of "turns within," beginning in Book XI and concluding in XIV, that carry the reader from reflection on ordinary sense experience, all the way into the innermost and non-adventitious immediacy of pure spiritual vision. The steps along this way are *conversiones* in two senses, conversion as change of mind, but also alchemical conversion, as in the conversion of lead to gold. They lead upward through a hierarchy of natures, to which the following programmatic statement refers:

> No doubt everything in the creature which is in any way like God, is not also to be called his image; but that alone than which he himself

alone is higher. For that only is in all points copied from him, between which and himself no nature is interposed.[81]

If a "nature" can be "interposed between" creature and God, natures must have something like rank, in hierarchical series. I list here the hierarchy of natures that Augustine has in mind, and will go on to sketch their role in *Trinity*.

spiritus	spirit
mens	mind
animus	thought
anima	soul
sensus	sense
corpus	body

Corpus, to begin at the bottom, is not *materia*. Matter is not even on the list, since it is less a nature than a decisive defect in the first nature: the corporeal or "bodily" nature. The body for Augustine belongs unquestionably to human being and is more than matter. It is an encumbrance to be sure, but not in the sense of attached baggage. The encumbering aspect of embodiment enters higher up in the stack, in the division against oneself in the soul that is called "concupiscence," and which is not a feature of the body as body. It is the living body, not the material object which our term "body" can also denote. It is matter gathered up into and already expressive of soul—in the arrangement of its organs, in its autonomic functions, its health.

But the hierarchy of natures does not place soul directly above body. The whole of Book XI, in which the paradigmatic phenomenological strategy for the rest of the argument is introduced, is an analysis of the second nature in our series, *sensus*, "sensuous consciousness." *Sensus* is not "sensation," by which we tend to mean discrete experiences separable from other, more proximate components of the field of consciousness (e.g., Locke's "simple ideas from sensation" in contrast to "ideas from reflection or the mind"). It is almost impossible to withhold from *sensus* the translation "consciousness," pure and simple. Augustine constantly

81. XI, 5, 8. CCSL L, 344; OT 149.

uses it in locutions like, *"O tu anima mea, ubi te esse sentis?"*[82] Since this question is addressed to the soul that sees itself before God, it will certainly not be answered by some "sensation." *Sensus* is far more striking for its "inwardness" than its function as a source of "input" into inwardness, which is the modern connotation. It has memory, and the freedom for an inner attention that can turn to memory. Both of these features parallel what in human *sensus* belongs to an "effigy" of the divine trinity, a first showing of the image of God.

The bottom three terms of the hierarchy schematize the possibility of a turn in the "outer man," sense turning within from body to soul. The top three schematize the possibility of a turn in the "inner man," mind turning from thought to spirit. Once again, the *anima/animus* complication that influences how Latin refers to the "rational soul" speaks to this outer/inner division.

In the natures I translate as "soul" and "thought" we find a pair that is indivisible in a special way. Soul and its thought, thought and the soul it lives with, are one in their twoness the way the man and the woman are two in one flesh.[83] Augustine finds the gender metaphor useful for several reasons; here, because the two are neither two nor one in such a way as to figure trinitarian relationships.

> When, therefore, we discuss the nature of human mentality, we discuss a single subject, and do not double it into those two which I have mentioned, except in respect to its functions. Therefore, when we seek the trinity in it, we seek it in the whole mind, without separating the action of the reason in things temporal from the contemplation of things eternal, so as to have further to seek some third thing, by which a trinity may be completed.[84]

Rising through the natures from below, arrival at the soul/thought complex is signaled by something in our dealings with corporeal nature

---

82. "o thou my soul, where dost thou sense thyself to be?" XV, 27, 50. CCSL L, 531; OT 227.

83. XII, 3, 3. CCSL L, 358; OT 156.

84. XII , 4, 4. CCSL 358; OT 156.

(therefore still involving sense) that adverts to the true and the good, thereby transcending the beast.

> These acts, and the like, although performed in reference to things sensible, and those which thought has deduced through the bodily senses, yet, as they are combined with reason, so are not common to men and beasts.[85]

What is here discovered, a life or nature bridging sense and reason, is not simple:

> For as among all the beasts there was not found for the man a help like unto him, unless one were to be taken from himself, and formed to be his consort: so for that mentality by which we consult the supernal and inward truth, there is no like help for such employment as man's nature requires among things corporeal out of those parts of the soul which we have in common with the beasts. And so a certain part of our reason, not separated so as to sever unity, but, as it were, diverted so as to be a help to fellowship, is parted off for the performing of its proper task. And as the twain is one flesh in the case of male and female, so one nature mentally embraces our intellect and our action, or our counsel and performance, or our reason and rational appetite, or whatever other more significant terms there may be by which to express them (e.g., *animus* and *anima*).

Continuing schematically, we come to *mens*. Mind is the capacity to hold the image of God in response to the gift of the Spirit of God. It is itself "spiritual" not as substance-thing in the sense of metaphysics, but precisely as a receptivity to inspiration. When the "powers" of the mind, its essential attributes, are at issue (reasoning, judging, etc.), Augustine vacillates between *mens* and *animus*. But when the receiving and holding of the image of God are discussed, he speaks only of *mens*—and it is in this context alone that the meaning of the mind's spiritual substance is decided. In the list of natures, *mens* is meant with this restriction; and only with this restriction will I hereafter use the English cognate "mind."

---

85. This and the citation to follow, XII, 2, 2. CCSL L, 357; OT 155.

Highest among natures is *spiritus*, for "God is spirit." When the two concepts "spirit" and "substance" are brought together by Augustine, at the conclusion of a phenomenological argument and as paradigm for much subsequent European philosophical psychology, it is spirit, guided by trinitarian hermeneutic of scripture, that modifies the concept of substance, not vice versa. Because of the trinitarian context, spirit is ontologically the more powerful concept in *Trinity*, to such a degree that substance in the case of spiritual substance takes on an entirely *sui generis* ontic meaning. If spirit is to be called "substance," it is the substance of the ecstasis involved in "having a future," and the ontology of such substance cannot be controlled metaphysically, whether the metaphysics be that of "substance" or "process."

I have followed the hierarchical list serially, but have indicated that it also schematizes two "turns," pertaining to the "outer" and the "inner" man: the turn in sense from body to soul, and the turn in mind from thought to spirit. Now it is the turn in the outer man in Book XI that provides the paradigmatic phenomenological strategy for the rest of the argument. The conversion here takes place in sense life. The basic memory/understanding/will format achieved in Book X is implemented here as retention/attention/intention.

Augustine has us consider sense in general by using the example of sight. When we are seeing something corporeal, three things can be distinguished: the visible aspect (the "look") of the corporeal thing, the vision in the sense, and the intention of the will (*intentio voluntatis*) holding the first in the attention of the second in such a way that they are conjoined as one. This unification is so complete that making the distinction will, Augustine expects, require hard reflection from many of his readers:

> . . . we cannot tell the form of the body we see apart from the form which is produced in the sense of the seer—not at least by the same sense, because the two coincide so exactly that there is no overlap to tell them apart by (*discernendens locus*).[86]

---

86. XI, 2, 3. CCSL L, 336; Trin. 305.

He knows a way to help those of "more tardy ingenuity" (*tardioribus ingeniis*) be more confident in granting the presence of an inner form.

> It often happens that when we look at some lights for a while and then close our eyes, certain luminous colors continue to revolve in our vision, changing their hues and gradually becoming less bright until they cease altogether. . . . the bars of window panes often appeared in those colors if our gaze happened to dwell on them. So that impression was there even while we were seeing, but it coincided so exactly with the form of the thing we were looking at that it simply could not be distinguished from it, and this is what our actual sight was (*et ipsa erat visio*).[87]

It is impossible of course that Augustine was the first person ever to have noticed the retinal afterimage, or the first to have taken pains to describe it. But this is the earliest context I know of in which such an observation becomes philosophically relevant.

The point of the discussion is to emphasize how accomplished and transparent is the unification of the visible and vision by the intention of the will. That unification is defective, however, inasmuch as the first two terms differ in nature. That defect is rectified if *the same intention* turns the attention of the sense away from the visible species of the thing and toward its retention in memory.

> Instead of the look of the body that was sensed outside, there now appears memory retaining that look which the soul drank in through the sense of the body; and instead of that external sight of the sense being formed from the sensible body, we now have a similar internal sight when the conscious attention (*acies animi*) is formed from what the memory retains, and absent bodies are thought about; *and the same will* (emphasis mine, *voluntasque ipsa*) that in the first case applied the sense for formation to the body presented to it outside and kept it joined to it as formed, now turns the conscious attention to the memory in an act of recollection for it to be formed from what the memory has retained, and there is produced in thought something like sight.[88]

87. XI, 2, 4. CCSL L, 337; Trin. 306.
88. XI, 3, 6. CCSL L, 340; Trin. 308.

The resulting vision is so little degraded that it sometimes does not allow even reason . . .

> . . . to judge whether a real body is being seen outside or something like it is being thought about inside.[89]

It is striking that Augustine makes hallucination the confirming heuristic for his claims about the inner image in vision.

Equally important for the argument is that "the look of a body outside" has been replaced by "memory retaining that look which the soul drank in through the sense of the body." After Husserl, the implied association of retention with the "look" of a body is familiar and natural. Augustine needed some intellectual calisthenics to make the same move directly,[90] but he wanted to describe the "conversion within" simply enough to make clear its situation in regard to natures. Because, now, the trinity of retention, attention, intention are all of the same nature. Compared to eyes-open seeing, they are "more inward" in a paradigmatic way.

What is paradigmatic here in Book XI, at the very first of the several conversions to follow, is the stress Augustine places on the *continuity* of the intentionality initially deployed in seeing with eyes open and the intentionality within. Again and again he says that they are the same. From the start of the whole project to unveil the image of God, the third term, the intention of the will, was always more inward and hence "higher" than the first two.

This leading role for the third term is the mark of the future in temporal problematic, and my warrant for learning from Augustine about "future" from temporal interpretation of his account of *will* in relation to memory and understanding in *Trinity*.

The generalization holds that the will acting on the upper/inward side of a conversation was always already active on the lower/outward side. And there is to some degree a kind of transitive carry-through, such

89. XI, 4, 7. CCSL L, 341; Trin. 309.
90. XI, 9, 16. "But I did not wish to propose a middle trinity in between, because it is not usually called a sight when the form that is produced in the observer is committed to memory." CCSL L, 353; Trin. 316.

that even at the early retention, attention, intention stage, the intention of the will is always already the pure love of the unveiled image of God, in its trinity of memory of self, understanding of self, love of self.[91] But here I come upon a deep problem for trinitarian theology, which I will only characterize but not pursue, to end the chapter.

In his sub-treatise on relations in God (Bks. V–VII), Augustine distinguishes terms that are proper to a divine relation from others that are "appropriated" to it. So, to be "word" is proper to the Son, but he is called "wisdom" by appropriation. But neither being "holy" nor "spirit" is proper to the relation of the Holy Spirit, since the Father is holy and is spirit, and the Son is holy and is spirit. Augustine therefore stands in need of a relation-term, sanctioned by scripture, for the Holy Spirit. He finds it in the word "gift." The Holy Spirit is the gift of God (*donum dei,* subjective genitive).

His question then becomes, is the gift of God also properly the love of God? It would seem that the scriptural saying, "God is love" (1 John 4:6) is speaking of essence/substance. But the pure love exposed in the image of God is a third term, temporally futural. The movement of the "more inward way" comes to a close in Book XIV, pointing into a final turn/conversion from creature to God. I return to the passages in Paul I cited at the start:

> Now we see in a mirror in an enigma, but then face to face (1 Cor. 13:12);

and

> But we all, with unveiled face, beholding-as-in-a-mirror (*katoptrizomenoi*) the glory of the Lord, are being changed into (*metamorphoumetha*) that same image, from glory to glory, as by the Spirit the Lord (*kathaper apo kuriou pneumati*) (2 Cor. 3:18).

The verb *metamorphoô* means "change," as in the English term "metamorphosis." The form here, *metamorphoumetha*, is first person plural, present, and either passive or middle. Translations are almost

---

91. XIV, 8, 11. CCSL LA, 436; Trin. 379.

invariably passive, "are being changed into," but in some ways construing it as middle better suits the theological issue here: "are changing into."

The problem is the character of the "agency" ascribed to the Spirit here. How does it relate to the pure love found in the image, whereby human being is "capable of God" (*capax deo*)? If that love is the gift of God (subjective genitive), then it will have been the Holy Spirit all along, leading within, that carried the human being before the mirror of enigmas, since "gift of God" is said properly of the third in the divine trinity.

As I said, I do not plan to take this question further in the context of Augustine's tools or arguments. All I will carry into the next, final chapter is a basic grasp of the unifying and transformative power of the future, in a temporal interpretation of divine trinity as the basis for the New Testament's understanding of revelation and prayer.

3. Trinity in the New Testament

SOMETHING IS A REVELATION only if it is revealing. Revelation is not a status but an impact.

The New Testament is an especially instructive instance of a revelation because it transpires to such a large extent in writing.

There continues to be rich and productive research into what happens when a living oral tradition passes over into documentation. But that belongs to historical research, and historical research is not the focus of this book. I am not proposing, for example, to contribute to the recovery of the historical Jesus.

As a revelation, the New Testament is not a depository of information about events prior to it, which themselves get taken to constitute the revelation, but is an emerging canon of works written in Greek, in whose complex intertextuality revelation is embodied. The revelation I am concerned with is the trinity of divine life, addressed in the New Testament as Father, Son, and Holy Spirit.

TRINITY IN REVELATION AND PRAYER

It is often but carelessly said that there is no trinity in the New Testament. They who make this charge are thinking of the "doctrine of the trinity," that nexus of disputes in an increasingly philosophical theology that starts taking shape in the third century, and becomes a treatise in the fourth and following centuries, with "trinity" taking on the sense of a title rather than a designation of revealed divine life.

Trinity in the latter sense is essential in the gospels, as can be seen from the prominence given to what I call the "baptismal icon." The latter is an icon, an image rather than a molecule of narrative, signaled by the different ways the evangelists present an essentially identical scene as being viewed. The icon itself shows Jesus rising from the waters of baptism as the new creation, recapitulating the rise of earth from primal waters in Genesis. Also shown is the heavens opened and the Holy Spirit descending upon Jesus in the form of a dove, completing the baptism with an anointing (whence Jesus is the anointed one, *ho christos*). Not represented is the voice of the Father, which is heard. (I have seen his words written below the icon as a caption, or lettered across the icon itself). In Mark, where it is Jesus who sees the heavens open and the Spirit descending, and to whom the words heard from heaven are addressed, they say: "Thou art my beloved Son; with thee I am well pleased" (Mark 1:11).

In Matthew, who is reading Mark, it is still Jesus who sees the Spirit descending like a dove and alighting on him. But where Mark stipulates as well that it is Jesus who saw the heavens opened, Matthew seems to make it more public by writing, "And behold, the heavens were opened" (3:16). This is confirmed by the words heard, which are now a public proclamation: "This is my beloved Son, with whom I am well pleased" (3:17). Luke's adaptation is complex:

> Now when all the people had been baptized, and when Jesus also had been baptized and was praying, the heaven was opened, and the Holy Spirit descended on him in bodily form, as a dove, and a voice came from heaven, "Thou art my beloved Son; with thee I am well pleased." (Luke 3:21–22)

Here the baptism of Jesus is not only subordinated to that of "all the people," but the icon itself attaches not directly to his baptism but to his being off praying. We no longer see him rising from the water—in liturgical perspective, a major revision of Mark. The words from heaven are addressed to him, as in Mark, but the open heaven, the dove, and the voice are all simply stated as facts, evident to no particular, identifiable viewpoint at all.

When we come to John's transformations of the viewpoint presented in the synoptics, they quickly introduce us to the effect the author wants his invocation of the baptismal icon to have. When John the Baptist sees Jesus approach, he proclaims, "This is the Lamb of God, who takes away the sin of the world" (1:29). He continues,

"I myself did not know him; but for this I came baptizing with water, that he might be revealed to Israel." And John bore witness, "I saw the Spirit descend as a dove from heaven. And it remained on him. . . . And I have seen and have borne witness that this is the Son of God." (John 1:31–32, 34)

More will be said below about the trinity features of the icon in John (the Father is "offstage"), but it is easily seen that the icon is now shown to John the Baptist. Its elements remain remarkably stable however: heaven, a descending dove, which alights on Jesus.

The placement of the baptismal icon early in the core narrative of the gospels—the story of Jesus from baptism to entombment, and its role in each case in the key theme of fulfillment of prophecy, refute the charge that there is no trinity in the New Testament. Intertextuality is also clearly illustrated in this example, though in a kind of brute force fashion that leaves unclear what I plan to accomplish by attending to it.

In an introductory step, let me outline with didactic brevity the structure of the two foundational dimensions of the New Testament to be explored in this chapter: revelation and prayer. These are intimately paired. If revelation is a divine initiative toward the human, prayer is the human response to that initiative, and a participation in it. I begin in the downward direction, with revelation.

God in the New Testament means the Father. The Father dwells in the abyss and is unknown. He is made known by the Son.

No one has ever seen God; the only Son, who dwells in the bosom of the Father, he has made him known. (John 1:18, RSV)[1]

But no one can confess that Jesus is Lord except by the Holy Spirit (1 Corinthians 12:3). This is the third moment in the structure of the revelation of God in Christ. If the Father and the Son count as one and two, then the Spirit is three—not by addition, but in a kind of involution that brings us back to one again. The Spirit is sent by the Father in the name of the Son (John 14:26). For this to be possible, the Son must go to the Father. In the parlance of the fourth gospel, he must be "raised up,"

---

1. Unless otherwise stated, I will use the RSV throughout.

which refers to the crucifixion and resurrection at once. So the Spirit is sent by the Father and the Son together, inasmuch as "I am in the Father and the Father in me" (John 14:10).

This "being-in" pertains not just to the Father and the Son. Via the Holy Spirit, it reaches as well those who are in Christ and no longer in the world. Referring to the day in which the world will no longer see him, Christ says:

> In that day you will know that I am in my Father, and you in me, and I in you. (John 14:20)

A few verses later, to reinforce his unity with the Father in being in us, he uses the first person plural, "we":

> If a man loves me, he will keep my word, and my Father will love him, and we will come to him and make our home with him. (John 14:23)

Chapter 14's whole presentation of the need for the Son to leave the world and go to the Father culminates in an anticipation of the sending of the Holy Spirit.

> These things I have spoken to you, while I am still with you. But the Counselor, the Holy Spirit, whom the Father will send in my name, he will teach you all things, and bring to your remembrance all that I have said to you. (John 14:25–26)

The Spirit consummates the revelation: "he will teach you all things. " It is not a stretch to associate the coming of the Holy Spirit with the "we will come" of the Father and Son, and indeed it is in just that role that Augustine holds the defining relation of the Spirit to be "gift of God" (*donum dei*).[2] The Holy Spirit is the divine *we*, "in person."[3]

Having set out to expound revelation as a divine initiative that reaches down to us, I come around to us caught up within it. The Spirit will

2. V, 14, 15.

3. Heribert Mühlen, *Der Heilige Geist als Person* (1963), was the first to refer to the Holy Spirit as "*das Wir im Person.*"

teach *you*, will remind *you*. If in divine life itself, the Spirit is gift, the identification of those to whom it is given requires they have a standing of some kind within divine life. It is precisely in prayer that this standing arises and shows its trinity-structure. Prayer is the arrival of the trinity, in its full vitality. I take each of them in turn. Prayer is *to the Father*. In the synoptic sayings source, he said to them . . .

. . . when you pray, say: "Father, hallowed be thy name. Thy kingdom come." (Luke 11:2, cf. Matthew 6:9)

In Luke's context, Jesus had himself been praying, and when he stopped, a disciple said to him,

Lord, teach us to pray, as John taught his disciples. (Luke 11:1)

The passage begins the Lord's Prayer. In Luke it is the Lord's in a twofold sense. The Jesus who teaches prayer has been addressed by the disciple as "Lord." But the scene also suggests that what the disciple asks is how to pray as Jesus himself has just been praying, so that it is his own prayer that he relates to them. And it is to the Father. Matthew achieves the fusion of Jesus at prayer with those who learn the prayer he teaches, directly, by beginning "Our Father . . ." (6:9). It is hard to imagine a more explicit and authoritative basis for saying that prayer is to the Father.

So it is *not to the Son*. This sounds perverse, as though one were denying the divinity of Christ. But the relationship of the believer to the Son in prayer is more intimate than that: prayer is *to* the Father, *as* the Son. Believers share his standing, first in that they themselves have become "children of God" (1 John 1:12, etc.; Romans 8:16, etc.), but second because joined in baptism to his dying and rising, they have become "one body" with him (Romans).

Prayer is also *not to the Holy Spirit*. The relationship of the believer in prayer to the Spirit is more intimate than that: prayer is to the Father, as the Son, and *in* the Holy Spirit.

When we cry, "Abba! Father!" it is the Spirit himself bearing witness with our spirit that we are children of God. . . . for we do not know how to pray as we ought, but the Spirit himself intercedes for us with sighs too deep for words. (Romans 15b–16, 26)

Prayer *itself* is the essential gift of the Holy Spirit, the opening of the human to the divine. In the Spirit, we receive standing to address the Father as a familiar, for we are children of God. The trinity of prayer is the trinity of revelation, lived from within.

My hope is that despite the declarative terseness of the foregoing, I will have made evident why the topic of this chapter, "Trinity in the New Testament," is a feasible one. What remains is to show in a more detailed way how temporal interpretation is the appropriate tool for unfolding the theme.

I have already brushed against a striking situation. Since Jesus says that the Spirit "will remind us" of everything he said, this has to include things that he *didn't say*—not "from the beginning" (John 16:4). Taking a familiar example of something he says in John, I ask, *when* does Jesus say, "Before Abraham came to be, I am" (John 8:58)?[4] In John, Jesus speaks in the office of the eternal Son, the glorified Christ. Conventional shorthand speaks of John having a "realized eschatology," presenting Jesus in a present that is really eternity. In Mark by contrast, Jesus is mainly presented passing between baptism and entombment, and Christ in glory lies in the future.[5] How to read Mark and John in the same New Testament, indeed how even to recognize their *theological* intertextuality, requires the insights of temporal problematic.

TRINITY AND TEMPORALITY IN THE OLD KERYGMA

To speak of the intertextuality of the books of the New Testament is to consider them all together, as a complete set of texts. I accept that implication, but not in such a way as to suppress the results of historical-

---

4. *prin Abraam genesthai egô eimi* (my translation). The RSV falters here (as do its predecessors going back to the KJV) by translating "before Abraham was, I am." But *genesthai* is an aorist infinitive, the tense for narrating past completed action, here "became," imperfect "was" is continuative, which undercuts the clash of temporal horizons in the saying, not to mention the contrast between the verbs for becoming and being.

5. The handful of exceptions are treated in the following section.

critical work, which at a minimum have demonstrated strata among the books, and sometimes within them, to which a rough chronological order can be ascribed.

Kêrygma means "proclamation, announcement," as distinct from, say, "teaching" (*mathêsis*) or "instruction" (*didachê*). Its prominence in early twentieth-century New Testament scholarship was anchored by the programmatic introduction of Jesus in the Gospel of Mark, coming back from the desert into which he was driven after baptism.

> Now after John was arrested, Jesus came into Galilee, preaching (*kêryssôn*) the gospel of God. (Mark 1:14)

As something to be proclaimed, the English word "gospel" itself was recovered in its root sense of "good news" (*eu-angelion*, *gôd-spell*, cf. German *gut-spiel*). Two things should be noted about this passage. First, Mark has earlier represented John the Baptizer as "preaching (*kêryssôn*) a baptism of repentance for the forgiveness of sins" (1:4). There is a strong implication that Jesus is not doing something altogether new, but picking up from John after his arrest. Second, this continuity becomes all the more striking when we look at the texts of what John and Jesus preach. John the Baptizer "appeared in the wilderness, preaching a baptism of repentance for the forgiveness of sins" (Mark 1:4).

> And he preached (*ekêrussen*) saying, "After me comes he who is mightier than I, the thong of whose sandals I am not worthy to stoop down and untie. I have baptized you with water, but he will baptize you with the Holy Spirit." (Mark 1:7–8)

Jesus likewise was preaching, saying:

> The time is fulfilled, and the kingdom of God is at hand; repent, and believe in the gospel. (Mark 1:15)

Both proclamations are apocalyptic, and both call for repentance in preparation for what is to come.

That John and Jesus have related, though different, roles for Mark, one bringing a time of preparation to conclusion, the other inaugurating a time of fulfillment, is announced at the outset (Mark 1:2–3), stitching together a verse from Malachi (3:1) and a verse from Isaiah (40:3) to make the transition something foreshadowed by the prophets. Far from diminishing the underlying continuity, this makes the move from the kerygma of John to the kerygma of Jesus the prototype for an equally consequential transition, that from Jesus to the church. Jesus preached the coming of the kingdom of God, the church preached Jesus— specifically, his death and resurrection. By the phrase "old kerygma," I mean to designate what is recoverable of the preaching of the church as it first arrives in the New Testament.

"First" here does not refer to the chronology of the New Testament writings. There are glimpses of old kerygma in the earliest writing, the authentic letters of Paul (e.g., the hymn cited in Philippians 2), that are less archaic than material incorporated much later (e.g., the speeches composed for Peter in Luke-Acts, especially Acts 2:14–36). The stratification I am interested in is not chronological but thematic. The example of Peter's speech in Acts 2 is especially valuable, because it expresses a Christology that is more archaic than that of Luke himself. One might try to use that fact to argue for the historical authenticity of the material, but I am much more interested in the fact that Luke's archaism is conscious, deliberate. It provides a baseline from which the distance his own position on trinity has traveled can be gauged. How then does trinity function in Peter's speech in Acts 2?

The scene is set immediately after a twofold manifestation of the Holy Spirit, in the sound of rushing wind in the house where 120 disciples were gathered for Pentecost, and in the vision of distributed tongues of fire resting on each of them (Acts 2:2–3). Because of the feast, the city of Jerusalem is full of Jews from all over the world. Luke calls the sending of the Spirit "the promise of the Father" (Acts 1:4; cf. Luke 24:49), and in the plan of Luke-Acts, it echoes the sending of the Spirit upon Jesus at the beginning of his ministry. The ministry now is that of the church, and Pentecost becomes the birthday of the church, whose success, miraculous in his eyes, is allegorized in the miracle of the tongues passage (Acts 2:6–12). Here the preaching of the church is heard in every country in its own language, but nothing about content is supplied. For the inaugural address of the church's mission, Acts brings forward Peter, standing with the eleven other apostles. In the passages to follow, I pare his speech down to its essentials for my purposes, setting aside references to the prophets and to David.

It begins:

> 22 "Men of Israel, hear these words: Jesus of Nazareth, a man attested to you by God with mighty works and wonders and signs which God did through him in your midst, as you yourselves know—23 this Jesus, delivered up according to the definite plan and foreknowledge of God, you crucified and killed by the hands of lawless men. 24 But God raised him up, having loosed the pangs of death, because it was not possible for him to be held by it."

The "men of Israel" are *andres*, and Jesus as well is an *anêr*, "a man" (i.e., not a god, nor a beast). He is an *apodedeigmenon*, someone pointed out, displayed, made known, by God. The agency of God is key throughout. The listed prodigies (*deigmata*, evidences) were all done by God "through him in your midst"; i.e., in this world, where life ends with death. The new proclamation concerning him is that God has now "raised him up" (*anestêsen*).

"Raised up" here (the Greek is identically ambiguous) conflates what for Luke himself are separate moments, elevations in a different sense: the bodily resurrection from the dead, and the ascension to the right hand of God. Peter briefly repeats the proclamation, and adds to it:

> 32 "This Jesus God raised up, and of that we all are witnesses. 33 Being therefore exalted at the right hand of God, and having received from the Father the promise of the Holy Spirit, he has poured out this which you see and hear."

"Of that we are all witnesses," is spoken *in the present tense. The preaching itself* is the witness, the evidence that Jesus has been exalted. He has sent the Spirit, the promise of the Father, pouring out "this which you see and hear."

But to what, precisely, does the "raising up" of Jesus refer? Unease over the imprecision, to a later ear, of the phrase "raised up" can become acute when the speech concludes using formal Christological titles:

36 "Let all the house of Israel therefore know assuredly that God has made him both Lord and Christ, this Jesus whom you crucified."

God "has made" (*epoiêsen*) him both Lord and Christ. As though he were not always Christ and Lord, since before creation even? The convenience of this formulation for what are later called "adoptionist" Christological heresies cannot be overcome by disambiguating the verb *poieô* here. Imprecision about the nature of the transition from Jesus, son of Mary, to Christ in glory seems to be characteristic of the old kerygma in general.

Consider Romans 1:3–4, where Paul is introducing "the gospel of God" to a church who do not know him. He expects the very archaism of the formulations he uses to testify to their authority. Collecting all the titles of Christ under the master title Son of God, here is what Paul says is the gospel of God:

> . . . the gospel concerning his Son, who was descended from David according to the flesh, 4 and designated Son of God in power according to the Spirit of holiness by his resurrection from the dead, Jesus Christ our Lord.

One can labor over how the contrast between "according to the flesh" (*kata sarka*) and "according to the Spirit of holiness" (*kata pneuma hagiôsunês*) should be understood, or to what degree the "by" (*ex*) in "by his resurrection from the dead" is causal/instrumental, but none of that has urgency compared to the enigmatic "designated Son of God in power" (*hosithentos huiou theou en dunamei*). Does the qualification "in power" mean in power only, and not in substance? Is "designated" even weaker than "made" in "made him Christ and Lord"?

There is as little to be gained by worrying the sense of the verb *horizô* here as there was with *poieô* above. At root it means to "divide, mark off, horizon." A determination of something by horizon (*horismos*) comes to mean "definition" in Aristotle. Has Paul said that Jesus is Son of God "by definition"? Would that be strong enough for orthodox Christology?

I have indicated already that Acts goes beyond the old kerygma by distinguishing between the resurrection and the ascension, and orthodoxy will eventually (in the Gospel of John) stipulate that Jesus

Christ was Son of God from the beginning (*en archê*), from before the creation of the world, so that anything whatever narrated about him in time is extrinsic to his status. This has the virtue of preempting ontologically any sort of adoptionism, but at the cost of rendering the whole of the gospel narratives superfluous.

As I see it, exposition of trinity in the Old Kerygma is thwarted when the questions pursued arise from narrative *sequence*, and transition and agency, explored as matters of *causality* in that context. For that context is always *time*, not temporality, and temporality concerns *disclosure*, not causality. In the Old Kerygma, a revelation is configured, a present is united with a past in an arriving future. There Trinity requires a *temporal* exposition.

Present is the Son in glory, at the right hand of the Father. *Past* is God's attestation for Jesus, and his "definite plan and foreknowledge" of his death. *Arriving* is the Holy Spirit, the "promise of the Father" for the future of the church, sent forth by the Son in union with the Father.

This temporal pattern does not belong to any particular time, but has the truth of Father and Son in the unity of the Holy Spirit, divine life itself, transcendently archaic, eternal, and free.

THE TEMPORALITY OF REVELATION IN MARK

The Gospel according to Mark was the first of the four narrative gospels in the New Testament to be written. Before Mark, "gospel" simply meant "good news." And the good news in the oldest Christian preaching about Jesus Christ was directly connected with what the Gospel of Mark tells us was Jesus's own good news:

> 1:14 Now after John was arrested, Jesus came to Galilee, proclaiming the good news of God, 15 and saying, "The time is fulfilled, and the kingdom of God is at hand; repent, and believe in the good news."

When, after his death and the experiences that led them to preach that "God had raised Jesus up and made him Christ and Lord," the disciples began proclaiming their own new insight into the "good news," it remained an essentially apocalyptic proclamation, one having to do with the imminent coming of the kingdom of God, and speaking out of a new and deepened confidence that "the kingdom of God is at hand." It was not shaped as a narration of the sayings and doings of Jesus.

In the narrative Gospels we reach a new stratum in the intertextuality of the New Testament, as I am signaling by capitalizing Gospel when I have in mind any of the four of them. Markan priority is important not just chronologically, but because two other Gospels (Matthew and Luke) share Mark as one of two principal sources in common. The three narratives can broadly be "seen together," and they are for that reason called the synoptic Gospels. It is not clear whether there were older narratives about Jesus that Mark drew from; this seems most possible for his account of the passion (Mark 14–15).

Agreement about Markan priority can devolve into an assumption that Mark is literarily primitive. As narrative, it is admittedly loose and lanky, regularly connecting two scenes with nothing more than the completely uninformative adverb *euthus* (straightaway, next). I would argue to the contrary that Mark is a crystal palace of formal structures.

One such structure is immediately evident; namely, the division of the text into two parts, pivoting around a strange two-stage healing of a blind man in chapter 8. This story is placed at the precise center of the sixteen-chapter Gospel. Among healing stories in all four Gospels, it is entirely exceptional. It is the only instance where it takes Jesus two tries to accomplish a healing.

This placement is important not just mechanically or dramatically but hermeneutically. What do I mean by the center of Mark? Mark ends at 16:8, with the women fleeing from the tomb and saying nothing to anyone.[6] If we take the numbered sixteen chapters to be compositional units, which they give every evidence of being, then the center of Mark would occur between chapters 8 and 9. But 16 is a stub, only 8 verses long (numbered verses are a medieval notation). That pushes the center back into chapter 8, where we do find it, in the two-phase healing of a blind man. Here is the passage:

8:22 And they came to Beth-sa'ida. And some people brought to him a blind man, and begged him to touch him. 23 And he took the blind man by the hand, and led him out of the village; and when he had spit

---

6. Verses 16:9–20 are a later addition, probably second century.

on his eyes and laid his hands upon him, he asked him, "Do you see anything?" 24 And he looked up and said, "I see men; but they look like trees, walking." 25 Then again he laid his hands upon his eyes; and he looked intently and was restored, and saw everything clearly. 26 And he sent him away to his home, saying, "Do not even enter the village."

No gospel story of the healing of a blind man is a medical miracle pure and simple. It is always an allegory as well, or a symbolical story of coming from unfaith (blindness) to faith (sight). Mark has placed it in the precise middle of his story, immediately after Jesus has chastised the disciples for their ignorance (8:17–21, ending with "Do you not yet understand?"), and immediately before the trip to Caesarea Philippi, which sees Peter stepping forward to confess that Jesus is "the Messiah" (*ho christos*) (8:27–30). It divides the Gospel into halves, each with its own agenda.

In the first half, often called the "Gospel of Power," Jesus is in public—proclaiming, teaching, healing, calling disciples, and defeating the demons and the whole kingdom of Satan. So when right after the healing of the blind man, Peter steps forward and says that Jesus is the Messiah, this is based only on what he has seen and been impressed by so far: all those signs of power. Mark represents Jesus as not fully accepting Peter's acknowledgement. He immediately begins teaching about the suffering Son of Man, and Peter won't hear it. Jesus rebukes him as on the side of Satan (8:31–33).

The second half of the Gospel—the "Gospel of Suffering"—shows Jesus mostly in private with his disciples, on the way up to Jerusalem and then undergoing his arrest, trial, and execution there. While he is shown teaching the disciples in the most explicit terms what must happen, they don't get it. Indeed, in the whole Gospel of Mark, no disciple of Jesus is ever shown reaching the full expression of Christian faith—that Jesus is the Son of God. The only human who testifies in these terms is a Roman Centurion (someone with whom the Gentile and probably Roman readers of the Gospel can identify) who says, after seeing the apocalyptic way in which Jesus has died, "Surely this was Son of God!" (15:39).

Peter has not come all the way in his confession, but he has come some way—allegorically half way. The movement in faith from blindness to vision requires two touches, the first from power (Christ), the second from suffering (the Son of God). Dramatically, and even historically, this is intelligible. Jesus was not easy to understand the first time around. For his disciples, the experience of realizing that something profound was going on with him must have begun as a glimmering of hope, but then came crushing catastrophe. Christianity was born in a "second time around" with Jesus, following his death, when the spiritual experience of the resurrection showed the memories his disciples had of the "first time around" in a new light. Mark's Gospel seems still in touch with what this was like for the disciples of Jesus. The ancient tradition that Mark was a disciple of Peter seems to me plausible.

In looking for the middle of Mark in the text itself, I noted that the final chapter 16 is a stub. It is short, and ends abruptly. Women have come to the tomb with spices to anoint the body of Jesus, but they find it already open and empty, except for a young man in a white robe who makes an Easter proclamation.

> 6 "Do not be amazed; you seek Jesus of Nazareth, who was crucified. He has risen, he is not here; see the place where they laid him. 7 But go, tell his disciples and Peter that he is going before you to Galilee; there you will see him, as he told you."

The women do go, but not to tell anyone anything:

> 8 And they went out and fled from the tomb; for trembling and astonishment had come upon them; and they said nothing to anyone, for they were afraid.

This seems a strange note on which to end his Gospel. In Greek, the final phrase "for they were afraid" is especially abrupt, *ephobounto gar*. To end a sentence with the postpositive particle *gar* is not normal. It is like a semantic poke in the eye. It creates a strong impression that something is missing, something has been left out. There are circles in which there is still talk of the "lost ending" of Mark.

Based on what the other synoptic gospels supply after the empty tomb (including the later Mark 9–20), what is missing is any appearance of the risen Christ. Proclamation of the dying and rising of Christ is what makes a Gospel gospel. For Mark, that proclamation is anchored by the title Son of God. From the very start, both author and reader know that Jesus Christ is the Son of God ("The beginning of the gospel of Jesus Christ, the Son of God," Mark 1:1). But as already noted, no human being within the story uses that title until the Centurion at the cross does so. Demons know it and say it, but Jesus tries to keep them quiet. The first instance of this comes in chapter 3.

> 3:11 And whenever the unclean spirits beheld him, they fell down before him and cried out, "You are the Son of God." 12 And he strictly ordered them not to make him known.

In critical discussion, this pervasive theme has been dubbed the "messianic secret," Mark deliberately delays human proclamation that Jesus is the Son of God until the right time, the moment of his death. But that still leaves us with a Gospel devoid of appearances of the risen Christ.

Or so it appears. To be specific, what are absent are appearances of the risen Christ *after* the empty tomb. As discussed earlier, for the Old Kerygma Christ "raised up" includes not only medically undead, but in glory. And there is a clear manifestation of Christ in glory in Mark, but *prior* to his death and burial: the transfiguration on the mountain. This comes in chapter 9, after Peter's confession, and when the fatal journey to Jerusalem has just begun.

> 2 And after six days Jesus took with him Peter and James and John, and led them up a high mountain apart by themselves; and he was transfigured before them, 3 and his garments became glistening, intensely white, as no fuller on earth could bleach them. 4 And there appeared to them Eli'jah with Moses; and they were talking to Jesus. 5 And Peter said to Jesus, "Master, it is well that we are here; let us make three booths, one for you and one for Moses and one for Eli'jah." 6 For he did not know what to say, for they were exceedingly afraid. 7 And a cloud overshadowed them, and a voice came out of the cloud, "This is my beloved Son; listen to him." 8 And suddenly looking around they no longer saw any one with them but Jesus only.

This is so expressly an epiphany of the Son of God in glory that it costs Mark some contortion to get the disciples down the mountain and back on the way to Jerusalem, where they will continue to be obtuse.

> 9 And as they were coming down the mountain, he charged them to tell no one what they had seen, until the Son of man[7] should have risen from the dead. 10 So they kept the matter to themselves, questioning what the rising from the dead meant.

Contemporary screenwriting and fiction can handle a flash-forward with greater sophistication, but Mark's maneuver is deft in its own way. It is not even clear that it is a flash-forward, a foretaste of the future exaltation to glory that will come after Jesus's death, since the ascension occurs only in Luke-Acts. The transfiguration is outside the main storyline not as future, but as a different kind of *present*, one that belongs

---

7. In all of the Gospels, Jesus is the only one who ever uses the phrase "Son of man." In Greek *ho huios tou anthrôpou*, it translates an Aramaic idiom that means simply a human being. It enters biblical literature in the apocalyptic vision in Daniel 7, where the figure of "one like a son of man" (7:13) is presented to "one like an ancient of days" (7:9), who is enthroned before the heavenly host on the day when "the books were opened" (7:10), the day of judgment. The figure is a human being, but seen in a heavenly manifestation, representing the "saints of the most high," the people of the new and everlasting kingdom that God would make in the age to come after the judgment of this world (7:14; cf. 7:27).

The problem for understanding how Jesus might have used the phrase is that while several times Mark shows him using it in classic apocalyptic contexts, (cf. Mark 8:38, 13:24–27, 14:62), the most important instances in Mark have to do with Jesus teaching the necessity of suffering for the "Son of man"—that is, for the one with authority to announce the coming of the Kingdom (cf. 2:10, 2:28). Three times in the second half of Mark's Gospel (8:31, 9:31, 10:32–34) Jesus confronts his disciples with this aspect of his announcement, but they won't hear of it and don't understand it. When Jesus is finally arrested, tried, and executed on charges of sedition by the Romans, his disciples are scattered and demoralized, as though caught completely by surprise.

The author of the Gospel according to Mark invested a major part of his creative powers in dramatizing the suffering servant aspect of the Son of man, which is not attested in the apocalyptic literature. That perspective may well have been Jesus's own.

to eternity, and only to time by participation. From a point of view like Luke's, Mark has looped appearances of the risen Christ back into the story of Jesus passing from baptism to entombment, but what he has accomplished is in fact quite different, and theologically more significant. He has provided a first sketch of orthodox Christology: the same Jesus passing from baptism to entombment *is* the Jesus Christ of glory. Neither Matthew nor Luke understands Mark's technique at this point, but the author of John does. He says in effect, if Mark can do a little of this, I can do it a lot. In John the eternal Son has all but completely crowded out the Jesus of the ministry, but in a way that Mark has foreshadowed.[8]

The temporal horizon for revelation in Mark is the present. To be sure, the transfiguration of memory wrought by the risen Christ is detectable in Mark, as is the historical future of persecution and suffering that overshadows its time of composition (ca. 66–70), but neither of these belongs to the fully temporal past or future as understood in this study. The full temporality of revelation is most fully evident in a comparison of Mark and John that takes into account their intertextuality, a task that needs a section of its own.

THE TEMPORALITY OF REVELATION IN JOHN

It is hard to overstate how drastically the portrait of Jesus walking and talking in the Gospel of John differs from that of Jesus in Mark. Characteristic of Mark's Jesus is that, as a healer, he appears to specialize in exorcisms. In John there are no exorcisms. In Mark, Jesus teaches in parables, indeed this is the subject of an entire chapter (ch. 4). In John there are no parables. Instead, we find dialogue in a highly developed format of a kind common in second-century gnostic "dialogues with the savior"—the ostensible difference being that in the latter, the savior is almost always the risen Christ, whereas in John it is Jesus between baptism and entombment. Finally, in Mark the focus of Jesus's teaching is the kingdom of God. But in John, instead of teaching about the

---

8. I believe there are additional epiphanies in Mark, most notably in the oddly redundant multitude feedings (6:34–44, 8:1–9), each followed by a boat scene (6:46–52, the walking on water; and 8:14–21, the disciples' failure). These are discussed below.

kingdom of God, Jesus teaches almost exclusively about himself, as eternal Son, and about his relationship to the Father.

The overall narrative is all but completely unconformable to the synoptic outline. What in the synoptics is the single, fateful and fatal trip to Jerusalem that ended his career—the one where he overturned the tables of the money-changers in the Temple courtyard—takes place in John near the very beginning of the story (2:13–16), and it is followed by two additional Passover visits. Those three Passovers are the sole basis for the conventional view that the public ministry lasted three years. Everything in Mark's story could fit between one Yom Kippur and a Passover, which would lend credence to his repeated reports on the disciples failing to grasp the meaning of the ministry the first time around. John's Last Supper is completely different from the synoptics' version, with no institution of the eucharist, but a seemingly unrelated ceremony instead (the washing of the disciples' feet), followed by four chapters of uninterrupted and highly theological discourse.

On the other hand, at the deepest level, where we ask what is it that makes a narrative be "gospel"—proclamation of the "good news" of what God has done in Christ—John is exactly like Mark. He portrays who Jesus is as the object of proclamation and faith ("Son of God"), matched with an outline of the nature and meaning of discipleship. In both gospels, Jesus is Son of God, but in Mark, whoever would follow him must "take up his cross" (Mark 8:34), while in John, the disciples are enjoined "to believe in" him. The meaning of the proclamation that Jesus is Son of God has shifted, but in what direction?

An especially far-reaching clue to the relationship between John and Mark comes from their handling of the trouble in soul that Jesus experienced before his passion. In Mark this takes place at a place called Gethsemane, and is set between the last supper and his arrest (Mark 14:32–42). The soul-trouble is vividly dramatized:

33 And he took with him Peter and James and John, and began to be greatly distressed and troubled. 34 And he said to them, "My soul is very sorrowful, even to death; remain here, and watch."

Before he goes on to quote Jesus praying, Mark summarizes the prospect that could cause him to sorrow to death:

35 And going a little farther, he fell on the ground and prayed that, if it were possible, the hour might pass from him.

Mark refers to the whole passion and death of Jesus, especially in its aspect of being the will of the Father, by calling it his "hour." At the end of the scene at Gethsemane, after he has prayed three times and each time found the disciples not keeping watch with him but asleep, his hour arrives, in the form of his approaching arrest.

41b "It is enough; the hour has come; the Son of man is betrayed into the hands of sinners."

This way of referring to the passion is solidified in the gospel of John. At the marriage feast at Cana, after his mother has drawn attention to the fact that the wine has run out, Jesus says, "Woman, what is this to me and you? My hour has not yet come" (John 2:4[9], my translation). In Chapter 12, which opens with widespread celebration of the raising of Lazarus from the dead, some Greeks (gentile proselytes) approach Philip saying, "Sir, we wish to see Jesus" (12:21). Philip, taking Andrew with him, reports this to Jesus, which triggers a long discourse that begins, "The hour has come for the Son of man to be glorified" (12:23). The reversal of Mark 14:41 is shortly exacerbated:

27 "Now is my soul troubled. And what shall I say? 'Father, save me from this hour'? No, for this purpose I have come to this hour. 28 Father, glorify thy name." Then a voice came from heaven, "I have glorified it, and I will glorify it again." 29 The crowd standing by heard it and said that it had thundered. Others said, "An angel has spoken to him." 30 Jesus answered, "This voice has come for your sake, not for mine."

In John, Jesus says, "Now is my soul (*hê psuchê mou*)[10] troubled." Taken along with the reference to "this hour," an allusion to Mark, who

9. Cf. also 8:20 and 13:1, "his hour."

10. That Jesus refers to his soul in John and Mark becomes very important in fifth-century Christological debate, because it establishes that in the incarnation, the human nature includes not just a body but a human soul.

had Jesus say, "My soul (*hê psuchê mou*) is very sorrowful" (14:34), is unmistakable. Yet here he goes on to say, "And what shall I say; 'Father, deliver me from this hour'?" That's as much as asking "What shall I say; shall I say the very thing you all know that I did say in the hour when I had trouble in soul?" And in Mark, after he prays to the Father for deliverance from "this cup," he is left derelict, not only with no answer from heaven, but abandoned as well by his disciples. Here though, the answer is "No!" (a strongly adversative *alla*, "but"), and instead, he as much as says, "Get it on!": "Father, glorify your name." A confirming voice is heard from heaven, which Jesus tells the crowd was for their sakes, not for his own.

The Johannine author was both aware of, and deliberately alluding to, the Markan scene. He was also expecting, even counting on, his readers to notice a *deliberate reversal of perspective*. I would argue that there is similar deliberation, and expectation, in the shifting of allusion to the liturgy of the eucharist in John from the Last Supper, where we find it in Mark (14:22–25), to much earlier in the Gospel, far from the whole passion context, in the feeding of the five thousand, followed by Jesus's walking on water (John 6:5–21, adapting Mark 6:34–52), which is where John locates the pivotal Bread of Life discourse (6:30–58; further discussion follows). We discover not just that John differs from Mark, but also that the author of John wants us to notice and think about the intentions behind those differences.

The last supper discourse is as central to the overall intentions of John as the passion is to Mark. Just as Mark can be called a passion narrative with an extended preface, so John is a meal discourse with an extended preface. The whole theology of revelation that controls the author's technique in the prior chapters is spelled out in chapters 14–17 (strictly speaking, the discourse begins at 13:31, where the thematic announcement is made: "Now is the son of man glorified"). The discourse that follows is that of the glorified = risen Son, heard "in the Spirit," saying the things that he "did not say from the beginning"—including that, and why, he did not say them. It provides the "logic" or *logos* that is "fleshed out" in the preceding chapters (cf. 1:1, "The *logos* became flesh and dwelt among us").

That "logic" is explicitly trinitarian. These chapters, in fact, provide more biblical texts supportive of later trinitarian theological developments than any other document in the New Testament. And temporal problematic is explicitly at work.

The argument of chapters 14 through 17 begins with Jesus explaining why he must "go to the Father" (14:13). It is so that the Spirit will be given:

16 "And I will pray the Father, and he will give you another Counselor, to be with you for ever, 17 even the Spirit of truth, whom the world cannot receive, for it neither sees him nor knows him."

After exhortation about keeping his word, stipulating, "The word which you hear is not mine but the Father's who sent me," he returns to the coming Counselor:

25 "These things I have spoken while I am still with you. 26 But the Counselor, the Holy Spirit, whom the Father will send in my name, he will teach you all things, and bring to your remembrance (*hupomnêsei*, remind you) all that I have said to you."

To explore the temporality of this disclosure of "all" ("all things," "all that I have said to you"), it helps to enrich its context with some of the redactional material inserted between chapters 14 and 18.

Chapter 14 ends with Jesus saying, "Rise, let us go hence," and the natural continuation comes at the beginning of chapter 18, "When Jesus had spoken these words, he went forth with his disciples across the Kidron valley, where there was a garden, which he and his disciples entered." The intervening chapters, 15 through 17, are redaction, perhaps in two stages. First, in chapters 15 and 16, the speech of chapter 14 starts up again and continues. Then in chapter 17, though still in the presence of his disciples, Jesus "raises his eyes to heaven" and addresses the Father (17:1) directly. I will take them up one at a time.

Chapter 15 begins with the image of Christ as the true vine, followed by the Johannine love commandment ("that you love one another as I have loved you," 15:12), and near the end comes again to the Counselor.

26 "But when the Counselor comes, whom I shall send to you from the Father, even the Spirit of truth, who proceeds from the Father, he will bear witness to me."

Then Chapter 16 goes on to expand the context for chapter 14's account of the work of the Spirit, to "bring to your remembrance (*hupomnêsei*, remind you) all that I have said to you."

> 12 "I have many things to say to you, but you cannot bear them now. 13 When the Spirit of truth comes, he will guide you into all the truth; for he will not speak on his own authority, but whatever he hears he will speak, and he will declare to you the things that are to come."

Why have Jesus specify that the Spirit "will not speak on his own authority"?

By the end of the first century, a particular kind of association of the trinity with past/present/future, one that will later be called the modalist heresy, had arisen. According to this, the mode of divine life called the Father was revealed in Old Testament history, that of the Son during the ministry of Jesus, and that of the Holy Spirit since Pentecost. The principle that the Spirit is sovereignly free, developed from "the wind (*to pneuma*) blows where it will" (3:8), is taken to mean that in the time of the Spirit (= nowadays), things will be revealed that go beyond what had been revealed previously, and these things will be thought suspect, unheard of. John rejects this directly when Jesus says that the Spirit will not speak on his own authority, "but whatever he hears he will speak." What the Spirit, sent from the Father and the Son, hears is the word (*logos*), which is spoken by the Son. In John, it will be a mark of any new thing heard "in the Spirit," whose status as revelation is secured by the Son, that *we must hear Jesus* speaking it.

The Spirit in verses 12 and 13 is temporally futural, an impending, an advent. His "will speak" is counterposed to "you cannot bear them now." The direct implication is that what the Spirit will speak, Jesus is *not saying now.*

> 16:4 "I have said these things to you, that when their hour comes you may remember that I told you of them. I did not say these things to you from the beginning, because I was with you."

"I did not say these things to you from the beginning," namely, from "when I was with you," when Jesus was with the disciples. In the immediate context, Jesus has just told them,

> "They will put you out of the synagogues; indeed the hour is coming when whoever kills you will think he is offering service to God." (16:2)

When the hour for these things comes, "you may remember that I told you of them." When were the disciples told of this hour? Well, "now," in this very speech. In John, Jesus is heard saying things that he did not say, including that he did not say them, and why. Yet when we hear them, we hear precisely Jesus saying them. I now return to the foundational passage for this puzzle, left pending above.

> "These things I have spoken while I am still with you. But the Counselor, the Holy Spirit, whom the Father will send in my name, he will teach you all things, and bring to your remembrance (*hupomnêsei*, remind you) all that I have said to you." (14:25–6)

The active, transitive force of "will remind you" (you is accusative in Greek) needs to be stressed. Jesus is in effect "remembered up," saying the things he did not say from the beginning. The Spirit who accomplishes this is sent by the Father in the name of the Son. The role of divine trinity in revelation for John is fully on display.

Temporal interpretation of this trinity must rule out modalism on principle. Past, present, and future are not regions of time, but horizons for the disclosure of historical existence, at all times. John has created a temporal disclosure space for his Gospel. What was latent in Mark, with his epiphantic looping of the risen Christ into the story of Jesus passing from baptism to entombment, is now in full bloom. The transition between Jesus speaking "from the beginning" to Jesus speaking in human exposure to the "spiritual future" takes place in our *hearing*, it is a *disclosure* event. For the reader, for whom the Gospel is a revelation, the disclosure is brought to life in prayer.

John's temporal disclosure is on display most fittingly in the Prologue, to which I turn next. An important passage in Acts throws light on two of its key concerns, the word and the beginning.

In Acts 10, Luke composes for Peter the first speech he makes to gentiles (Cornelius and his entourage), and it is the first one to go beyond proclamation to include narration of the sort found in the gospels. Indeed, it begins with a recognizable digest of the synoptic plot outline. I cite its two opening verses:

> 36 You know the word which he sent to Israel, preaching good news of peace by Jesus Christ (he is Lord of all), 37 the word which was proclaimed throughout all Judea, beginning from Galilee after the baptism which John preached.

Two things are to be noted: the subject of the narration is "the word" (*ho logos*), and pains are taken to identify its "beginning" (*arxamenos apo*, beginning from). Recall that Mark opens with an assertion about "the beginning": "the beginning of the gospel of Jesus Christ the Son of God" (*archê tou euangeliou Jêsou Christou huiou theou*). In the Prologue with which John opens, "beginning" is handled in a way that is a tacit rebuke to Matthew and Luke, who do not follow Mark in beginning their narratives with the prophetic anticipation and coming of John the Baptist, but rather preface his coming with two chapters of (very different) nativity stories. In the Prologue, John includes Mark's beginning, but he interweaves it with another beginning as well, that of Genesis. He says in effect, "If you want to make another beginning than Mark's, don't go reaching back to the holy family, or through genealogy to David or Abraham or even Adam, but make the *big* beginning, the 'in the beginning' of Genesis."

In the accompanying presentation of John 1:1–23, I put the verses comprising the Prologue proper, the theological introduction, in a column on the left, and those that open the narrative of Jesus from baptism to entombment on the right. The verses are presented in order, but each column is coherent in itself. If one begins reading John with the right-hand column, John makes Mark's beginning. If with the left, one encounters a profoundly self-contained proclamation of the eternal Son. With this signal of John's interweaving of eternity with time, I close this section.

1 In the beginning was the Word, and the Word was with God and the Word was God. 2 He was in the beginning with God; 3 all things were made through him, and without him was not anything made that was made. 4 In him was life, and the life was the light of men. 5 The light shines in the darkness, and the darkness has not overcome it.

6 There was a man sent from God, whose name was John. 7 He came for testimony, to bear witness to the light, that all might believe through him. 8 He was not the light, but came to bear witness to the light.

9 The true light that enlightens every man was coming into the world. 10 He was in the world, and the world was made through him, yet the world knew him not.
11 He came to his own home, and his own people received him not. 12 But to all who received him who believed in his name, he gave power to become children of God; 13 who were born, not of blood nor of the will of the flesh nor of the will of man, but of God.
14 And the Word became flesh and dwelt among us, full of grace and truth; we have beheld his glory, glory as of the only Son from the Father.

15 John bore witness to him, and cried, "This was he of whom I said, 'He who comes after me ranks before me, for he was before me.'"

16 And from his fulness have we all received, grace upon grace. 17 For the law was given through Moses; grace and truth came through Jesus Christ. 18 No one has ever seen God; the only Son, who is in the bosom of the Father, he has made him known.

19 And this is the testimony of John, when the Jews sent priests and Levites from Jerusalem to ask him, "Who are you?" 20 He confessed, he did not deny, but confessed, "I am not the Christ." 21 And they asked him, "What, then? Are you Elijah?" He said, "I am not." "Are you the prophet?" And he answered, "No." 22 They said to him, "Who are you? Let us have an answer for those who sent us. What do you say about yourself?" 23 He said, "I am the voice of one crying in the wilderness, 'Make straight the way of the Lord,' as the prophet Isaiah said."

THE TABLE FELLOWSHIP OF JESUS

I have argued that the Gospel of John has displaced its reference to the eucharist from the last supper, where it is found in Mark, moving it away from the passion. I have yet to address the question, however, of *why* John puts where it occurs, in the long "bread of life" discourse in chapter 6. The eucharistic reference is unmistakable in these lines:

> 6:51 "I am the living bread which came down from heaven; if any one eats of this bread, he will live for ever; and the bread which I shall give for the life of the world is my flesh." 52 The Jews then disputed among themselves, saying, "How can this man give us his flesh to eat?" 53 So Jesus said to them, "Truly, truly, I say to you, unless you eat the flesh of the Son of man and drink his blood, you have no life in you; 54 he who eats my flesh and drinks my blood has eternal life, and I will raise him up at the last day."

This is incomprehensible apart from the blessing of the bread in the liturgy of the eucharist, whose wording in Mark is "Take; this is my body."[11] The Greek word for "body" is *sôma*. This is very general. It can denote the human body, but also any other material thing, living or not. It would not be used of food at a meal; but *sarx*, "flesh," would be, for a serving of meat (including the meat of fruit). To tell someone to "eat my flesh" would sound appallingly graphic, and that is just what John 6 reports:

> Many among his disciples said, "This is a hard saying; who can listen to it?" (6:60)

The word "body" that became traditional in the liturgy may be the triumph of a euphemism. In any case, it is apparent that the words of the blessing of the loaf in the Johannine eucharist were "This is my flesh."[12]

---

11. Paul, "This is my body which is for you" (1 Cor. 11:24); Luke, "This is my body which is given for you" (22:19). Matthew adds, "Take, eat" (26:26).

12. Here and elsewhere in this section, I benefit from Raymond Brown, *The Community of the Beloved Disciple*. Paulist Press, 1978.

But why pronounce them where John does, in chapter 6? The chapter opens with a retelling of the first of two multitude-feeding/boat-scene sequences found in Mark, the one where five thousand are fed leaving twelve baskets of leftovers (Mark 6:34–44), followed by the boat scene where Jesus comes to his disciples walking on the sea (6:46–52). Here is how Mark tells it:

> 48 And he saw that they were making headway painfully, for the wind was against them. And about the fourth watch of the night he came to them, walking on the sea. He meant to pass by them, 49 but when they saw him walking on the sea they thought it was a ghost, and cried out; 50 for they all saw him, and were terrified. But immediately he spoke to them and said, "Take heart, it is I; have no fear." 51 And he got into the boat with them and the wind ceased. And they were utterly astounded, 52 for they did not understand about the loaves, but their hearts were hardened.

The disciples are terrified, utterly astounded. They did not understand, their hearts were hardened. But it was not the walking on water or the sudden ceasing of the wind that they did not understand: "they did not understand about the loaves," i.e., something about the feeding of the five thousand.

In the second sequence, where four thousand are fed leaving seven baskets of leftovers (Mark 8:1–9), the subsequent boat scene makes what they fail to understand more precise.

> 14 Now they had forgotten to bring bread; and they had only one loaf with them in the boat. 15 And he cautioned them, saying, "Take heed, beware of the leaven of the Pharisees and the leaven of Herod." 16 And they discussed it with one another, saying, "We have no bread." 17 And being aware of it, Jesus said to them, "Why do you discuss the fact that you have no bread? Do you not yet perceive or understand? Are your hearts hardened? 18 Having eyes do you not see, and having ears do you not hear? And do you not remember? 19 When I broke the five loaves for the five thousand, how many baskets full of broken pieces did you take up?" They said to him, "Twelve." 20 "And the seven for the four thousand, how many baskets full of broken pieces did you

take up?" And they said to him, "Seven." 21 And he said to them, "Do you not yet understand?"

What they do not see, hear, or remember is the number of baskets of broken pieces they collected! The reader can be left as baffled as the disciples. This takes some work.

When the feedings are represented in this way, the heart of the "miracle" is the impossibility of breaking indefinitely many pieces large enough to be nourishing from a single loaf of bread. But to consider the feedings naturalistically in that way is finally comic, as many film directors have discovered. It plays like the circus stunt where impossibly many clowns climb out of a single car. And the texts themselves speak against it.

There is a formality in the feeding in Mark 6 that has the eucharistic liturgy in view.

> 39 Then he commanded them all to sit down by companies upon the green grass. 40 So they sat down in groups, by hundreds and by fifties. 41 And taking the five loaves and the two fish he looked up to heaven, and blessed, and broke the loaves, and gave them to the disciples to set before the people; and he divided the two fish among them all.

Fifty and a hundred approximates the size of early house churches. Jesus's actions parallel those in Mark's last supper, where he "took bread, and blessed, and broke it, and gave it to them" (14:22). The same gestures recur in chapter 8, closing again with the disciples being given the bread "to set before the people" (8:6). The seed of the doctrine that the eucharist recapitulates the last supper has been planted.[13]

Returning to the boat scene in chapter 8, the actual statement by Jesus to which the disciples are so obtuse is "beware of the leaven of the Pharisees and the leaven of Herod." The Pharisees are the teachers of the Jews, Herod a paradigm of power among the gentiles. Together they

13. Eucharist means "blessing," "giving thanks," and is the word cited by Paul for the liturgical gesture in 1 Cor. 11:23. Mark uses it in the second of his multitude feedings, *eucharistêsas* (8:6). In Mark 6:41, "he blessed" is *eulogêsen*, and this is what Matthew (26:26) and Luke (9:16) follow.

betoken the whole world.[14] Likewise the numbers the disciples fail to understand, twelve and seven. Twelve is the number of the tribes of Israel, seven (the seven wonders, etc.) points to the gentile world. In its superabundance, the bread over whose blessing Jesus presided, and to whose distribution at meals he assigned the disciples, has enough left over for Jews and gentiles alike—for the whole world.

I call this the apostolic eucharist. About it Paul writes, "As often as you eat this bread and drink the cup, you proclaim the Lord's death until he comes" (1 Corinthians 11:26). It is a eucharist of recollection and anticipation, taking place "between the times." Its liturgy is called the Lord's Supper. For the bread that comes down from heaven in John 6, the bread of life in its soteriological function, the liturgical name is "communion" (*koinônia*).

So I return to the eucharist of communion, even incorporation, in John 6. There the first verse of the bread of life discourse is, "Truly, truly, I say to you, he who believes has eternal life" (6:47). This is said in the present tense, as is, "he who eats my flesh and drinks my blood has eternal life" (present tense, 6:54a). This aspect of Johannine theology is sometimes called "realized eschatology." It would be an exaggeration to say that John is devoid of apocalyptic eschatology; verse 54 just cited continues, "and I will raise him up at the last day." But eternal life here and now is by far the most prominent aspect of Johannine communion. Stated in the liturgical formula "he who eats my flesh and drinks my blood," "believing in" Jesus was the crux of the dispute that rent the historical Johannine community. A Johannine elder, writing later to combat "false prophets" whose spirit is not "of God," states what marks the "Spirit of God":

> By this you know the Spirit of God; every spirit which confesses that Jesus Christ has come in the flesh is of God. (1 John 4:2)

Given the Gospel's rejection of nativity stories, the only Johannine context available for the freighted term "flesh" is the eucharistic one. What is at stake in believing the incarnation is *communion*, about which

---

14. Matthew in his parallel misses this; he has Jesus say, "Beware of the leaven of the Pharisees and the Sadducees," (16:6), making it a matter internal to Judaism.

the author of 1 John is even more intense than the Gospel. "God is love, and he who abides in love abides in God, and God in him" (4:16). Commonality with God is reciprocally interior.

I will not conclude without exploring the implications of this line of thought for the Prologue formula, "the word became flesh and dwelt among us," but to do so seriously, the problem of the historical discipleship of Jesus cannot finally be evaded. My proposal is that the foundation of the New Testament is the table fellowship of Jesus, in which the temporal disclosure space of revelation was primordially opened. For access to that experience, one final and complex intertextual situation must be delineated.

I bring us to Q, the synoptic sayings source (*Quelle*, German for "source"), a Greek document that we do not have, but which is nonetheless an authentic stratum of the New Testament. It is the other principal source, along with Mark, that is shared by Matthew and Luke. The security with which its text can be recognized in joint citation can be judged from the following logion. For critical reasons that need not be rehearsed here, Q is conventionally first cited from Luke, in this instance, Luke 10:

> 10:21 In that same hour he rejoiced in the Holy Spirit and said, "I thank thee, Father, Lord of heaven and earth, that thou hast hidden these things from the wise and understanding and revealed them to babes; yea, Father, for such was thy gracious will. 22 All things have been delivered to me by my Father; and no one knows who the Son is except the Father, or who the Father is except the Son and any one to whom the Son chooses to reveal him."

Matthew 11 has:

> 11:25 At that time Jesus declared, "I thank thee, Father, Lord of heaven and earth, that thou hast hidden these things from the wise and understanding and revealed them to babes; 26 yea, Father, for such was thy gracious will. 27 All things have been delivered to me by my Father; and no one knows the Son except the Father, and no one knows the Father except the Son and any one to whom the Son chooses to reveal him."

Differences in this case are very small: Luke says no one knows "who the Son is" and "who the Father is," Matthew just "the Son" and "the Father." Otherwise, the two versions are identical. The passage consists of two sentences whose relation to one another is not immediately evident, but what leaps from the page is that the second sounds like the Gospel of John. This is the only place in the synoptic Gospels where Jesus uses "the Father" and "the Son" elliptically, as he does in the Gospel of John, rather than "the Son of God" or "the Son of man." And the theology of revelation is Johannine: "All things have been delivered" to the Son; the Father and the Son have reciprocal knowledge of one another; and the Father is revealed "to any one to whom the Son chooses to reveal him." In the nineteenth century, Karl von Hase called this "a meteorite fallen from the Johannine sky,"[15] and meteorological characterizations have become entrenched. Today it is often called the "Johannine thunderbolt."

The opening sentence is a *berakah*, a benediction or prayer of thanksgiving to God used in synagogue liturgy or on solemn occasions. Louis Bouyer has recognized it as an ancient *berakah* for wisdom.[16] God has "hidden these things" from the wise and understanding "and revealed them to babes," and it is hard not to hear that as "babes such as these"; i.e., Jesus is speaking in the presence of his disciples. Such a benediction would be natural at an occasion of table fellowship, such as a meal. In the Jewish meal liturgy of Jesus' time, there was an opening benediction over a cup of wine to be shared, which amounts to a call to table, and then a benediction over bread that puts the meal in session: after the bread has been passed, one can no longer join the fellowship. The meal ends with a triple benediction in which God is called upon to remember his faithfulness to his promises, those to Abraham, to Moses,

15. Karl von Hase, *Geschichte Jesu. Nach academischen Vorlesungen*. Leipzig, 1876, 421–23. Reference from an online paper by Adelbert Denaux, "The Q-Logion Mt. 11,27 / Luke 10,22 and the Gospel of John," 3http://www.academia .edu/5371617.

16. *Eucharist: Theology and Spirituality of the Eucharistic Prayer* (Paris, 1966), translated by Charles Underhill Quinn. University of Notre Dame Press, 1968, especially chs. 2 through 5.

and those still pending. It is not as though God might forget his faithfulness, but we who are reminded, in giving thanks for it.[17]

In seeing the Q logion as eucharist liturgy, my argument is not just from generic Jewish table practice, but also from the centrality of its closing proclamation for the eucharist itself—but for the Johannine eucharist, not the synoptic. This is just the aspect that makes the passage a meteor.

My assumption is that elliptical reference to the Father and the Son is authentic to Jesus, but not understood in the old kerygma and synoptic traditions. The representation of the Gospel of John's hero (a "beloved disciple" carefully not named in contrast to Jesus's famous named companions: Peter, Andrew, James, etc.) as someone who understood Jesus better than the others may be historically valid. The Q passage, seen in its full intertextuality, convinces me of that.

This has important implications for the temporality of a pivotal feature of eucharistic liturgy, the *anamnêsis* (remembrance). We find this in Luke 22:19, attached to the blessing of the bread, "Do this in remembrance of me (*eis tên emên anamnêsin*)."[18] Remembrance is often taken in the sense of a memorial: "That one exceptional table blessing, the night before I was arrested; repeat this henceforth as my memorial." I think the sense is different: "This thing we have been doing all along, *keep doing that.*"

What had they been doing? In the table fellowship of Jesus, in *koinônia*, they had been experiencing an advent of knowledge, having the veils pulled back from their eyes, the scriptures coming clear. I don't imagine Jesus teaching in the sense of declaiming, making himself the center of discourse, but rather as posing and taking questions. It was an occasion for the arrival of wisdom. When, after his death, they returned to the table of his blessing, *the same thing kept happening.*

"The word became flesh and dwelt among us" in a most concrete and definite way, in the table fellowship of Jesus. As *anamnêsis*, the eucharist is the basis for the two key propositions of Christology, resurrection and

17. Luke has two cup blessings, 22:17, before the bread; and 22:20, after supper, suggesting he is aware of Jewish meal liturgy.

18. Paul attaches it to both the bread and the wine (1 Corinthians 11:24–25). Because of his two cups, Luke keeps it with the single blessing of bread.

incarnation. Etymologically, the word is *ana*, (back, again), plus *mnêsis*, (minding, present in mind). The temporal determination of the eucharist is the present, but the present of a particular temporal past, the table blessing of Jesus. Having found this in the logion from Q, where it is the risen Christ who is speaking, the "flesh" of his benediction is the "flesh" of John's Prologue. So the word becomes flesh in the eucharist.

This can be confirmed from the liturgy. What is the referent for "this" in "this is my body" and "this is my blood"? The traditional answer is the bread and the wine themselves, as substances, hence the doctrine of "transubstantiation." My assertion is that "this" is the bread *as broken and passed around*, the cup *as shared*—hence the table fellowship itself.

The New Testament shows that eucharistic fellowship was the future for the discipleship of Jesus from the beginning, and this includes the historical discipleship. Eucharistic "bearing in mind" is how we got from the New Testament church to Jesus. But there is no reason to suppose that the temporal disclosure space has closed. The table fellowship of Jesus still has a future today.

BIBLIOGRAPHY

Augustine. *Confessiones*. The text is accessible in vols. 26 and 27 of the Loeb Classical Library. Harvard University Press, 1912, also widely online. *Confessions*, translated by Henry Chadwick. Oxford University Press, 2009.

———. *De musica*. A critical edition is available only for Book VI, Stockholm: Almqvist and Wiksell, 2002. The text of all six books is available online in the Thesaurus Musicarum Latinarum at the School of Music, Indiana University: http://www.chmtl.indiana.edu/tml/3rd–5th/3RD–5TH_INDEX.html.

———. *St. Augustine on Music*, Books I–VI, translated by R. Catesby Taliaferro. St. John's Bookstore, 1939. Also in *Saint Augustine: The Immortality of the Soul, the Magnitude of the Soul, on Music, the Advantage of Believing, on Faith in Things Unseen*. Catholic University of America Press, 1977.

———. *De trinitate libri quindecem*. Corpus Christianorum Series Latina, volumes L (Books I–XII) and LA (Books XIII–XV). Brepols Publishers, 1968. *On the Trinity*, translated by A. West Hadden, edited and annotated by W.G.T. Shedd. Nicene and Post-Nicene Fathers, volume III, 1–228. Grand Rapids: Eerdmans, 1956. *The Trinity*, translated by Edmund Hill. New City Press, 1991.

Bouyer, Louis. *Eucharist: Theology and Spirituality of the Eucharistic Prayer* (Paris, 1966), translated by Charles Underhill Quinn. University of Notre Dame Press, 1968.

Brown, Raymond. *The Community of the Beloved Disciple*. Paulist Press, 1978.

Heidegger, Martin. *Der Begriff der Zeit* (1924; lecture and monograph expansion). Gesamtausgabe 64, edited by F.-W. Herrmann. Vittorio Klosterman, 2004. The lecture, to the Marburg Theological Society, "The Concept of Time," is translated in Kisiel-Sheehan, *Becoming Heidegger*. The monograph has been translated as *The Concept of Time: The First Draft of Being and Time*, translated by Ingo Farin. Bloomsbury Academic Publishers, 2011.

———. *Die Grundprobleme der Phänomenologie* (summer 1927). Gesamtausgabe 24, edited by F.-W. Herrmann. Vittorio Klosterman, 1975. *The Basic Problems of Phenomenology*, translated by Albert Hofstadter. Indiana University Press, 1982.

―――. *Phänomenologie des Religiösen Lebens* (winter 1920–21). Gesamtausgabe 60, 1995. *The Phenomenology of Religious Life*, translated by Matthias Fritch and Jennifer Anna Gosetti-Ferencei. Indiana University Press, 2004.

―――. *Sein und Zeit* (1927). 12te Auflage, Tübingen: Max Niemeyer Verlag, 1972. *Being and Time*, translated by John Robinson and Edward Macquarrie. Harper & Row, 1962.

Kierkegaard, Søren. *Begrebet Angest* (1844). *The Concept of Anxiety*, edited and translated by Reidar Thomte and Albert B. Anderson. Princeton University Press, 1980. Also *The Concept of Dread*, translated by Walter Lowrie. Princeton University Press, 1957.

Kisiel, Theodore. *The Genesis of Heidegger's Being and Time*. University of California Press, 1993.

―――. *Becoming Heidegger*, edited by Theodore Kisiel and Thomas Sheehan. Northwestern University Press, 2007.

Manchester, Peter. *The Doctrine of the Trinity in Temporal Interpretation*. Ph.D. dissertation, Berkeley: Graduate Theological Union, 1972. University Microfilms, 72–33, 344.

―――. *The Syntax of Time*. Leiden and Boston: Brill, 2005.

Plotinus. *On Eternity and Time*, Ennead III 7. Translated by A. H. Armstrong. Plotinus volume 3, Loeb Classical Library 442, 1967.

―――. *Nature, Contemplation, and the One*, Ennead III 8. As the above, Loeb Classical Library 442.

TeSelιe, Eugene. *Augustine the Theologian*. Herder and Herder, 1970.